6/81

Event and interpretation

EVENT AND INTERPRETATION

Henry Wansbrough OSB

Sheed and Ward · London

First published 1973
Sheed and Ward Ltd, 33 Maiden Lane, London WC2E 7LA
© Henry Wansbrough 1973

Nihil obstat: John M. T. Barton STD, LSS *Censor*
Imprimatur: David Norris *Vicar General*
Westminster, 7 May 1973

This book is set in 11/12 Baskerville
Made and printed in Great Britain by
Eyre & Spottiswoode Ltd,
at Grosvenor Press, Portsmouth

CONTENTS

PREFACE

Most of the chapters contained in this volume were originally published in *The Clergy Review* in the years 1967-1971 under the title 'Event and Interpretation'. The purpose of these articles was to investigate how the deep meaning which events in their history had for Israel, and events in the life of Christ for the evangelists, have affected their presentation in the old and new testaments. The authors of the books of the bible had no interest in presenting historical events as though with the disinterested eye of the outsider; their accounts betray freely the vivid faith and warm concern with the past events which had shaped their religious history and continued to live on in them till the present day. Fused into their accounts, then, is their view of the importance of these events in the life of Israel and of Jesus. Modern man, however, who no longer moves in the same thought-world, can learn much both about the actual events and about their significance by attempting to distinguish these two, and by looking at history and theology separately. It is this which these articles attempted to do.

In this series there was nothing on the resurrection, so it seemed fitting to complete the picture with three articles written for *The Way* in 1971/2. The angle here is slightly different, for the articles were published under the title 'Theological Trends', and designed first to investigate what was being said by contemporary theologians about the event of the resurrection before going on to discuss the presentation by each of the gospel writers.

To the editors of both periodicals I am most grateful both for permission to publish the articles in book form and for the criticisms they made in the course of the original publication.

H.W.

Abraham our father

Only with the greatest difficulty can we grasp that the kingdom of heaven is like a grain of mustard seed. Automatically we measure the importance of an event from the notice or excitement which it arouses. Even physical greatness helps: for Westerners it is easier to believe that de Gaulle was a great man than to grant that Shastri was. The people of Israel too shared this tendency, to such an extent that we are constantly tempted to suppose that the major figures of biblical history played a major part on the stage of history. It is with aggrieved surprise that we discover that ancient records bear no trace of Abraham, the exodus or the crucifixion, that these are shadows which have vanished without trace from the classic screen of history.

How can these two presentations of history be so different? Which is the 'true' version, that found in the ancient Egyptian and Mesopotamian texts and in the Greek historians, or that found in the bible? In this age of historical criticism, when the student is constantly encouraged to return to the objective, unbiased contemporary sources, one would be tempted, in the search to discover what actually happened, to grant the preference to the non-biblical sources; they, after all, have no axe to grind. But any historian worthy of the name has an axe to grind; he selects and presents events according to a pattern which he sees, according to interests which he has. Even the chronicler must make a choice among the myriad 'events' which occur during the period which he wishes to chronicle, and in his description select, from among the myriad facets which go to make up the event, those which he considers significant. The difference between the modern and the biblical historian is that the modern historian presents, beside his (already biased) description of events, the theory which he considers the account to illustrate; the reader may therefore, in judging the theory, demand a restatement of the events which were presented in such a way as to accord with it. The biblical author, however, makes no attempt to separate event and interpretation. For one reason, he wrote at a time before the evolution of the concept of 'objective history'; before every man demanded the right to judge the account for himself. For a second reason, the interpretation of the biblical author is the inspired interpretation, the view of history which God wished to be set before his people, which was no doubt, indeed, already the view of his people, crystallised over the course of many generations.

For the modern historically critical mind there is, however, a desire to separate out event and interpretation. This is not necessarily the result of doubt about the author's interpretation, for the desire is shared by the most faithful believer in the inspiration of the bible. Nor is it due merely to idle curiosity to know 'what actually happened'. It is rather that we feel that by serving up event and interpretation on two different dishes we may gain more from each of them, may both come nearer to sharing the experiences of our fore-fathers in the faith, and penetrate more deeply the message which the inspired author conveys by his way of describing the event. One man may wonder at the appearance of perfect symmetry and harmony which the Parthenon conveys; another may admire the knowledge of optics and geometry which caused the ancient Greeks to employ assymetry in precisely the way which would convey such an impression. The former attitude is that of simplicity, the latter that of the analytical mind.

Abraham was a great man, the father of the chosen people, the 'friend of God' (as the Muslims still call him). He is the great example of faith, who left his people and his country in reliance only on the promise God gave him. From the bible we certainly gain the impression that he was a king among kings, slightly inferior perhaps to Pharaoh, but at least on terms of intimacy with him. With his army of retainers he put to flight the four kings of the East who had routed the five kings of the cities of the plain.

A first reaction of the critics, on discovering the difference between this and the records of secular history, was to deny all existence to Abraham. He was a personification of some tribal god, or the concretisation of the primitive tribe itself, invented many centuries after the dramatic date of the events in which he figures, at the court of King Solomon. But subsequent research and discovery has reinforced the minute conformity with history of many of the stories of Abraham. A number of details provide illustrations in practice of ancient Near Eastern legal prescriptions, as we find them in the great semitic codifications of laws, in the private contracts found at Nuzi on the Euphrates, or in Hittite legal documents. These details must have been faithfully handed down, long after their significance was forgotten, as the sagas of Abraham were retold by his descendants. Even the names of Abraham and his family have their parallels in the documents of the period; many of them recur exactly in the records of the early second millennium, others are of a type well known at that time. Significantly, they show that Abraham came from a family whose chief deity was the moon; this was, indeed, to be expected, for the moon has a special place among the gods of Ur in Mesopotamia.

Not only the details but also the general trend of the story stand against a background which has been filled in by recent discoveries. The wanderings of Abraham were part of a general movement of migration from Mesopotamia through Palestine and eventually into Egypt, under the pressure of ethnic movements from the Arabian desert. Abraham and his family, a clan wandering with their flocks of sheep and goats, would have been typical of such nomads; they are still found in Palestine today, staying in one place any length of time from a few days to a month before loading their belongings on to their beasts of burden, to move on to other pastures. Now, as then, they avoid the more fertile cultivated areas. Egyptian records show that there were already a number of towns in Palestine, and a still more developed tribal organisation.

But the story of Abraham shows that he kept to the border areas between the cultivated land and the desert, where the rainfall is just enough to provide meagre pasture for flocks and herds. In times of drought these nomads still move down into the well-watered Nile delta; Egyptian records of all periods show that it was always the last resort of the parched nomads.

Abraham is not, then, a stately and solitary figure,

wandering alone through the land which is to belong to
his descendants. He is one of many nomads who passed
unnoticed through the land with their black tents of
goat hair. The promise to possess the land was not for
him but for his descendants. He receives no more than
the burial plot which he buys at Hebron — again
typically of nomadic tribes, whose one fixed point is the
family burial plot to which they bring back their dead.
In what way, then, was he special? What was there
heroic in his following the path of so many others? It is
Abraham's great age which is constantly stressed in the
story, and the impossibility of his wife Sarah bearing
children. An ageing nomad is dependent on his children
for his support and livelihood; his whole hope lies in his
children. Without children he can at best hope for some
meagre support from his more distant relations. Yet it is
without children that Abraham sets out to follow God's
promise — a situation without hope or prospect —
turning his back on the one chance of survival in old
age.

Nor had he the comfort of a well-developed theology,
a full notion of the mercy and goodness of God. The
revelation of God's name itself was still to come, at the
time of exodus. The revelation of his nature was to
continue throughout the bible, but the first decisive
revelation does not occur before the exodus. When
Abraham's servant or his son refer to the God who
protects them and guarantees their prosperity they can
give no fuller description than 'the God who appeared
to Abraham'. We must avoid attributing to Abraham the
comfort of our own theology, of our own knowledge of
God's dealings with his people. This historical perspective requires a degree of abstraction of which the

biblical authors were not capable; at any rate they did not attempt it. God is the same always, and they have no interest in stressing the progressive discovery of his nature; they presume in Abraham the knowledge of their own time. Abraham, however, had no knowledge of God's fulfilment of his promises; on the contrary, the fulfilment seemed ever longer delayed, ever more difficult of accomplishment. It was in the darkness of faith in the virtually unrealisable promise of a practically unknown God that Abraham set out on his journey into seeming annihilation.

This is the central core of the Abraham story; the sagas which were collected round him illustrate this theme. Most of the sagas were handed down in two slightly different versions, one (the so-called Yahwist tradition, which uses this personal name for God even before it is revealed to Moses) stemming from the southern kingdom of Judah, and concentrating on stories linked with that area, the other, which gained written form only some two centuries later, brought by exiles from the northern kingdom of Israel, and representing the traditions of the northern tribes. Not all were perhaps originally told of Abraham himself: the story of the abduction of the patriarch's wife and his canny trick for regaining her is related of Abraham in both traditions. But it ill accords with the stress on Sarah's age and barrenness (according to the present arrangement of the story she is ninety years old when the king of Gerar is tempted to lay hands on her, Gen 17:17; 20). The same story is told of Isaac and the king of Gerar; we may suspect that it was to Isaac that the story originally belonged — it is linked to him also by the pun on his name (26:8) — and was attached to

Abraham only secondarily. The transference of the story well illustrates the character of the tales of Abraham: they are sagas told about the great ancestor of the people of Israel and, as with all stories about the great founders of communities, it does not matter too much to which of the founders some of the stories are attached.

It is also from this story of the abduction of the patriarch's wife that much of the impression of Abraham's political importance is drawn, for he parleys with the king, and receives handsome gifts from him (12:16; 20:14). But the term 'king' is an elastic one; every village has its king (cf Jos 12). During the period of semitic rule in the Egyptian delta no doubt many local princelings could claim the title of pharaoh, though the title could also be explained by the gradual elevation of village headman to pharaoh in the course of constant retelling of the story. The same explanation may hold of the enigmatic campaign of Abraham against the four kings in Gen 14, since the attempt to identify them with known historical figures has now been abandoned; they may represent a group of sheikhs raiding from the desert. We can draw no conclusions about the size of their forces from the 318 members of his household with whose help Abraham routs them, for this figure corresponds to the numerical value of the letters of his servant Eliezer's name.

In other cases the sagas around Abraham are primarily ethnological. The story of the dismissal of Hagar (16:6-15; 21:8-21), localised as it is to a well in the desert of the Negeb, is really the story of the origin of the tribe of the Ishmaelites, and of their relation to Israel. A better-known example of such a story is that of

the supplanting of Esau (or Edom) by Jacob (or Israel);
the relations between the two hostile nations, related by
blood but strongly divergent in character, are described
in terms of their progenitors. In the same way many of
the priestly genealogies of the book, which appear to us
to catalogue the descent of persons, are in fact
composed of the names of tribes and towns, expressing
the ethnological or political groupings of these rather
than that of individuals. But the great age of the story
of Hagar is shown by its accordance with the details of
the legal rights of a mistress over a slave-girl whom she
gives to her husband as a substitute in the case of her
own barrenness, as we find them in the texts of the
mid-second millennium (cf *Ancient Near Eastern Texts*,
ed J. Pritchard, 1955, p 220). The story is too closely
bound up with Abraham's personal drama, representing
a moment of impatience in his waiting for the accomplishment of the promise, to be dismissed as a mere
accretion.

The importance of Abraham is neither ethnic nor
political but religious, as our father in the faith, the first
member of the chain of men to whom God made
himself known, at first with an experience which was
only a promise, finally by the revelation of his Son. His
response was the paradox of faith, setting off to
hopelessness in hope. This is the historical content of
the Abraham tradition, handed down in the sagas of
Israel.

2

Desert encounter

The impression of the first events in the life of Israel as a people, the exodus from Egypt, the covenant of Sinai and the entry into Canaan, which most people retain from their reading of the bible — or more often of 'bible stories' — is of a triumphant march through the desert by an immense host, carrying all before it, stopping at Mount Sinai to pick up a copy of the law, and then sweeping on to annihilate the Canaanites. It is a sort of 1967 Israeli-Egyptian campaign in the opposite direction. Was there not the crushing series of blows which were the ten plagues? Did not the sea stand as a wall at the passage of Israel (Ex 14:22) while pharaoh was drowned? Did not 603,550 fighting men set out from Egypt (Num 2:32), representing total numbers in the region of two million? Did not Moses receive the words of the law already engraved on tablets of stone? The sceptic, whether believer or not, is sorely tempted to reply to all these questions in the negative; he may be restrained by the conviction that he would be doubting God's word. It is not the possibility of the miraculous that the believer doubts; he only asks whether all this proliferation of the wonderful was necessary and consistent with the sober guidance of the universe which we know. This distaste for the wonderful as, at best, a kind of ostentatious vulgarity is a comparatively recent phenomenon. Before the advent of rationalism it was taken for granted that almost the only criterion of God's presence and action was the miraculous: the more saintly a man, the more miracles he must work — a correlation which seems to us today far from self-evident. This explains not only why such narratives were never questioned before, but also to some extent their genesis.

The Hebrews were an oppressed rabble of Asiatics; the name, spelt in various ways, is not primarily racial but denotes more a situation; it is used of mercenaries, prisoners, slaves, hirelings and bandits (eg 1 Sam 14:21; Ex 21:2). In Egyptian texts they were chiefly prisoners of war, some 800 of whom are known to have worked in the lethal quarries of Sinai under King Ramses IV. As P. Barthélemy has pointed out (*Dieu et son image*, 1963, pp 75-6) God waited till there was a syndrome of circumstances which threatened a group with extermination — a racial minority in the midst of a totalitarian state with the means to exterminate it and motives for doing so — before choosing and saving a people for himself. They would then owe their life totally to him. It is this saving intervention by God, when all hope of survival seemed gone, that Israel remembered.

It was a marvellous intervention, and as Israel realised ever more deeply how marvellous it had been, this was expressed by a proliferation of the marvellous in the stories which surrounded it. There is no word in the biblical vocabulary which corresponds to our word 'miracle' with its popular connotation of an event contrary to nature. Israel had no such precise concept of nature or the laws of nature, and so could not think in these terms, drawing a careful line between an extra-ordinary natural occurrence and one which was clean

contrary to nature; if such happenings are clearly part of
God's plan, and so caused by him, they are all 'the
wonderful works of God'. Thus when we puzzle over
whether the plagues were *supernaturale quoad essentiam*
or only *quoad modum* we are making a distinction of
which the authors of the stories were not even dimly
aware, and posing a question which we cannot expect
them to answer. If we are to understand the narratives
we must read them from the point of view of the
authors.

The ten plagues were, first and foremost, signs of
God's power and choice to save Israel. But they were
not always ten. The narrative falls in a part of the
Pentateuch where the work of the different authors or
schools of authors is most intricately interwoven. The
number ten results from a conflation of the sources (the
final editor frequently puts two traditions of the same
event side by side, eg Gen 15 and 17): the mosquitoes
of the third plague clearly double the gadflies of the
fourth, and the cattle-boils of the sixth no doubt double
the cattle-plague of the fifth. Of the two older sources
one (the Elohist) seems to have had only five plagues,
while the oldest of all (the Yahwist) had seven. This
number, which denotes completion, is a favourite of his;
the possibility is immediately raised that he filled out
the number of plagues to seven to show the complete-
ness with which God afflicted the Egyptians. It is
remarkable (J. A. Barucq, DBS fasc 42, 1967, 12) that
in the introduction to the section on the plagues in
Exodus only two signs are mentioned. The first, some
water drawn from the river turning to blood when it is
poured on the ground (Ex 4:9), is intended to convince
the stiff-necked Israelites. There is perhaps a trace of

this more modest sign in the account of the first plague, for Moses' miracle is imitated by the royal magicians, which could hardly have happened if all the water in Egypt had already been turned into blood. The narrative is complex, composed from all three major sources, and shows an increase in the extent of the miracle as the sources get later. In the Yahwist's account only the river is affected; the Elohist expressly says other water was still drinkable (7:24). But the priestly writer insists that all the waters of Egypt 'even down to the contents of every tub or jar' (7:19) were tainted. But is even the Yahwist-Elohist version affected by this tendency to increase the marvels which is so evident in later writings? Did he combine the original sign with the well-known natural phenomenon of the reddening (or rather browning) of the Nile waters during the flood season?

The other sign which God promises to enable Moses to perform is the foretelling of the death of the king's first-born (4:23). The accomplishment of this threat is extended to all the first-born of Egypt (12:29). But here again later influence may be suspected, for this plague is joined to the command to offer all the first-born of Israel, man and beast, to Yahweh (13:1, 11-16). Since these two are connected in the cult and in men's minds (though the offering of the first-born is descended from a custom far older than the exodus: R. de Vaux, *Institutions de l'Ancien Testament* II, 1965, pp 329-30) there may well be some contamination which has caused the generalisation of what was originally a single case. There remains the difficulty that we have no record of the sudden death of the eldest son of the pharaoh at this time. A safe solution is the appeal to the fragmentary and reticent character of contemporary Egyptian records. But a more realistic solution is the appeal to the popular nature of the stories in the bible. It has already been remarked that 'king' is an elastic term (p 7): here it may be used for the ultimate overseer of these Hebrew slave-gangs. This solution may apply also to the difficult problem of the drowning of the 'chariots and horsemen of Pharaoh's whole army' (14:28). If the 'king' is in reality a local overseer, delegate of the king himself, then the absence from historical records of the annihilation of his armed force is less difficult to explain.

If it be granted that a basis in certain wonderful signs by God has been magnified by popular love of the amazing in telling stories, but still with relation to the well-known and striking vagaries of nature in Egypt, the way is open to explaining how the Yahwist arrived at his number of seven plagues. The occurrence of reddening of the Nile floodwaters, of freak hailstorms, of locusts and of darkness during a *hamsin* has long been used by apologists: God employed these basically natural phenomena, but the miracle consisted in their opportune occurrence and their unusual extent. If we approach the problem from a literary point of view we may say it was the biblical writer who made use of these natural phenomena to express the drastic nature and complete effectiveness of God's action.

The sea of reeds

The same reasoning cannot be applied to the crossing of the 'Red Sea'. The location of this sea is impossible to establish; much later (in 1 Kg 9:26) the name is applied to the Gulf of Aqaba, but it is hard to believe that the Egyptian force pursued that far. Nor may we deduce its position from knowledge of the route followed, for there seem to be two different traditions on this matter, one bringing Israel by a northern, possibly coastal, route, the other leading the people deep into the Sinai peninsula. But, wherever it was, the name, correctly translated 'Reed' or 'Papyrus Sea', suggests shallow water. The account of the crossing (14:15-31) is again composite, and again the late priestly writer increases the marvellous: instead of the Yahwist's strong east wind all night, for the priestly writer the cause is Moses' outstretched hand (14:21a) — no secondary causes allowed; and the water, instead of being merely driven back, forms walls to right and left of them (14:22). M. Noth(*Exodus*, 1962, p 116) insists that 'it must remain uncertain what [the Yahwist] meant to express', objecting that no sirocco could dry up even a shallow sea: he curiously suggests that the account reflects the experience of a mirage. But the difficulty comes from insistence on absolutely dry land. If we accept that already the Yahwist had a tendency to inflate the marvellous element, then the classic explanation of the well-known phenomenon of a strong wind lessening the depth of the water to make it passable, till it returned to clog the wheels of the Egyptian chariotry (14:25), is perfectly acceptable.

In all this a major difficulty of the biblical accounts is the immense number of fighting men given, which turns what otherwise seems to be the escape of a party of fugitive slaves into a mass migration, where flight before the Egyptian force and such a crossing of the sea are equally unlikely. The experience of being lost in the Sinai desert without water has helped to convince the present writer that the fugitives cannot have constituted more than a large clan; there is simply not enough water. Various attempts have been made to explain the 603,550 of Num 1:46; 2:32; it has been suggested that *'elef* (=thousand) here means 'family' or 'clan', as in Jg 6:15; 1 Sam 10:19. But it may be questioned whether even 600 families is not too much. The most satisfactory explanation again takes into account literary factors: the priestly author of Num 2:1-2, whose historical perspective was less demanding than ours, simply inserted census figures of his own time, drawn probably from some temple count (cf Ex 38:26). His justification for doing this was the quasi-definition, that all Israel came through the desert, and encountered God on Sinai. In one sense this is historically false, for all through the wanderings Israel was gathering supporters and adherents: as they set off a miscellaneous rabble joined them (Ex 12:38); later a clan related to Moses by marriage links its fortunes with his (Num 10:29-32); by the time they have reached the desert of Paran (Num 13) they have been joined by a group of Kenizites under Caleb. One may see how this snowballing took place, and why, from Num 10:29-32 and from the great pact at Sichem in Joshua 24, the primitive version of which seems to have recounted the alliance of the non-Israelites of Sichem with the Israelites. In each case the non-Israelites recognise that Yahweh is a great God who guards his people; they choose him as being an effective patron, under whose banner a people will find protection and prosperity. This was a world in which a god must prove himself in order to win and keep adherents;

this Yahweh had done by taking his people from Egypt and gradually increasing their strength from a handful of fugitive slaves to a horde who could obtain a foothold among the much more advanced peoples of Palestine. The non-Israelite became an Israelite by joining himself to this victorious and growing people, by taking Yahweh for his god, and taking upon himself the history of this people and the obligations of their covenant with God. It is in this sense that all Israel had crossed the sea, marched through the desert and encountered Yahweh on Sinai.

Sinai

The great event of the exodus and wanderings, to which all others lead or from which they flow, was the encounter with God on Sinai. It is difficult now to penetrate to the historical reality of this event; not only is it related in two different places (Ex 19 and 34),but 'the important central section of the tradition of the theophany on Sinai has frequently been worked over and provided with expansions' (Noth, *op cit,* p 154). Whatever was the sensible form of this encounter with God, it was expressed in terms of earthquake and thunderstorms, terms which became normal in the biblical vocabulary for expressing God's presence and intervention among his people (eg Jg 5:4-5; Is 2:10-21; Mk 13:8; Mt 27:51). The central place which this experience of God held among his people is shown not only by the origin of the imagery in which encounters with God are ever afterwards described, but by the concept of God which was there formed. For it was on

Sinai that God first revealed the meaning of his mysterious name, Yahweh. In spite of the Septuagint translation 'I am who am', expressing the nature of God in Greek terms meaningless, or indeed unthinkable, to the Hebrews, scholars now tend to regard the Lord's statement to Moses in Ex 3:14 more as a refusal to explain his nature or to reveal himself, a mere codeword by which to refer to the 'God of your fathers'. The exegesis of this name comes only in Ex 34:6 ff when God himself interprets it, revealing himself as 'a God of tenderness and compassion slow to anger, rich in kindness and faithfulness', This revelation of God's mercy is quoted or alluded to again and again in the prayers of the old testament (Jer 32:18; Jl 2:13; Jon 4:2; Ps 86:15, etc), showing how basic it was to Israel's spirituality.

In legal terms this meeting between God and Israel which was to shape all Israel's history was expressed in two ways, the covenant and the law. Ancient treaties between a king and vassal peoples before and until, but not after, the time of Moses are known which contain the principal elements found in the covenant formulae: a preamble in which the king names himself (Ex 20:2a: I am Yahweh your God) and proclaims the benefits which he has already conferred on the vassal (Ex 20:2b: who brought you out of the land of Egypt). There follow the conditions on which the king will protect his vassal, foremost among which is the condition that he shall remain sole overlord (Ex 20:3: You shall have no gods except me). Finally there is often the prescription that a copy of the treaty shall be preserved in the sanctuary, as were the stones of the law (Ex 25:16, cf *Ancient Near Eastern Texts,* ed J. Pritchard, 1955, pp

202-5). This is why Yahweh's love for his people is expressed so often in the prophets in terms of the love which comes from a covenant relationship, such as that of husband and wife.

The law

The Pentateuch would seem to imply that the other legal way of expressing the consequences of this encounter with God, the law, was brought down by Moses fully formed after his sojourn on the mountain. This is of course an oversimplification, another of those foreshortenings of which we have already met quite a number. In one sense again the law is indeed wholly given on Sinai because it is the consequence of that encounter, the working out of the necessary conditions of being the people of God and associating with him. When first the ancient codifications of law were discovered in the last century, and it was seen that a large proportion of the prescriptions contained in the law of Israel were drawn either from them or, more probably, from the same background, considerable scandal ensued. But though the material prescriptions may be drawn from such human sources of experience and legislation, their sanction is wholly different; only in Israel is the binding force of law expressed in theological terms dependent on the revelation of Yahweh: 'Be holy as I am holy'.

In fact it can now be clearly seen that there are, broadly speaking, three codifications of law in the Pentateuch, which can be distinguished by the circumstances of the people for which they legislate. The first, the so-called code of the alliance (Ex 20-23), is the most interesting, reflecting as it does an agricultural and pastoral society, and formed from a series of judgements which may well go back — though as a whole it is to be dated in the period of the judges — to the years spent by Israel at Ain Qadesh (also called the Well of Judgement) before the entry into the promised land. It is hardly fanciful to see here the trace of those first judgements given by Moses and his elders (Ex 18:13-26) when they were first working out the consequences of their encounter and alliance with God.

The events which we have here discussed were so central to Israel's very existence that piety and a certain natural mythopoeic tendency inevitably allowed the bare outlines of events to be obscured by their interpretation. But if there were no firm historical nucleus of these the Jew could say, as the christian of the resurrection: 'then is our faith vain'.

3

Israel at the walls of Jericho

The people shouted, the trumpets sounded. When they heard the sound of the trumpet, the people raised a mighty war cry and the wall collapsed then and there. At once the people stormed the town, every man going straight ahead, and they captured the town. They enforced the ban on everything in the town: men and women, young and old, even the oxen and sheep and donkeys, massacring them all. (Jo 6:20-1.)

This picture of the taking of Jericho and its bloody consequences has stirred the imaginations of poets and musicians down the ages, and the consciences of more recent christians. It symbolises the sweeping advance of Israel like a tidal wave, rolling all before it and annihilating all obstacles, until the fury of the flood subsides into calm possession of the terrain by a single people devoted to Yahweh and oblivious of the horrors it has perpetrated. But was the advance in fact so sweeping, and was it so bloody?

It has long been recognised that this picture, inspired by the Book of Joshua, is a radical oversimplification. It is contradicted in the bible itself by the admissions of Judges (1:18-35) that much of Palestine resisted the invasion of Israel. Many of the fortified Canaanite towns held out for centuries: Jerusalem itself remained a Jebusite stronghold, blocking the main hill road between northern and southern tribes, until captured by

David (2 Sam 5:6-12). The division between north and south was reinforced by Canaanite Gezer, a few miles to the west of Jerusalem, until it was captured by the pharaoh and given to Solomon as a dowry (1 Kg 19:16). A reading of the conquest stories in Joshua 2-10 map in hand shows that they concern only the territories which belonged to the tribe of Benjamin. They are the stories of the entry of this tribe into possession of their land. Other tribes were less fortunate (Jos 13:1-6; 17:12, 16).

Unrest and invasion

The Israelites were, despite their faith and successes on the material plane, a primitive people. Nomads or semi-nomads as they were, they would have little chance of assaulting the strongly fortified towns of Palestine (until the invention of gunpowder, capture of fortified towns by assault was rare, for it was easier to defend than to attack). Nor could they compete with the chariotry and horses of the peoples of the plain (Jos 17:16). Their chance lay in exploiting the unrest attested by archaeology for Palestine between 1400 and 1200, and in joining in with the attacks on the settled population made in this period by their cousins, the Habiru or 'Apiru (= Hebrew). The signs of unrest are multiple: at the end of the fifteenth century Egypt was losing control of her possessions, or more exactly client princes, in Palestine and Syria. For the period 1370-53 we have a series of letters written to Pharaoh Akhenaton from the princelings of Palestine who remained loyal to him, begging his help. The enemy most frequently mentioned in these letters — called the

Amarna letters because they were discovered in
Akhenaton's record office at Tell el-Amarna — are the
'Apiru. Some of the 'Apiru, at any rate, were disaffected
slaves (Letter 288), and thus in the same class as the
Habiru of the Egyptian records, ie the Hebrews of the
bible. In the Amarna letters they are in league with a
certain Labayu and his sons, who are recorded as having
given the land of Sichem to the 'Apiru (Letter 289),
together with a fair amount of other territory. It is
tempting to see some connexion between the presence
of the 'Apiru in Sichem recorded here and the great pact
at Sichem in Joshua 24. Certainly the conditions created
by these disturbances, uncontrollable plunderings and
seizure of land would be ideal for the related nomads
who came in from the East.

The evidence of Palestinian cities confirms this
picture. During the whole period the culture is at a
considerably lower level than before, no doubt due to
the constant war and dislocation. Most cities so far
excavated show at least one destruction during this
period (cf K. Kenyon, *Archaeology in the Holy Land,*
1965, pp 209-18). Jericho seems to have been abandoned c 1325; Tell Beit Mirsim (=? the Kiriath-sepher of Jos
15:15-16) was sacked c 1350 and again c 1230.
Similarly Bethel was burnt once in the fourteenth and
once in the thirteenth centuries. Megiddo was destroyed
c 1350 and again during the thirteenth century. Lakish
survived intact until the end of the thirteenth century.
There are, then, two main moments of destruction; the
first may well be associated with the 'Apiru. The second
coincides roughly with a punitive expedition of Pharaoh
Merneptah in 1230, in which he claims to have laid
waste a number of Palestinian cities (*Ancient Near*

Eastern Texts, ed J. Pritchard, 1955, p 378). But the margin of error in such datings does not exclude the possibility that the cities had at the time of this expedition already been sacked by the Israelites. Indeed the one people, as opposed to city or country, which is mentioned in the hymn celebrating Merneptah's victory, is Israel. The people of Israel were, then, a force in the land, though not yet in sufficient control or sufficiently sedentary to deserve classification as a city or district.

Previous occupation

Independent evidence shows, therefore, that the bible presents the happenings of the entry of Israel into Canaan too much in isolation; the Israelites cashed in on a general movement. But is there not some trace in the bible of these other 'Apiru who were already in Palestine c 1370-53? Genesis contains some mysterious stories about the patriarchs, which seem to suggest some sort of intermarriage with the local population long before the entry under Joshua. They are no more than scraps of reminiscence: Reuben's union with Bilhah, his father's concubine (Gen 35:22), the rape of Dinah and Simeon and Levi's treacherous revenge (Gen 34), Judah's marriage with a Canaanite woman (Gen 38:2). O. Eissfeldt (*Cambridge Ancient History* II, ch 26a, 1965, p 12) suggests that we should consider these stories 'as preceding by a considerable period the land settlement linked with the names of Moses and Joshua'. Since such stories of intermarriage in ancient folklore never concern merely individuals but always represent an event or series of events which concern at least a

large part of the tribe, there may well have been
elements of the Israelite people already in Canaan at the
time of the return from the exodus. Indeed this
statement hardly does more than give from the biblical
angle the same view as was indicated by the archaeo-
logical evidence for the 'Apiru. In a previous chapter we
saw that not all the Israelites came out of Egypt with
Moses; on the march through the desert and Transjordan
there was a continuous snowballing movement. Now it
appears that there were Israelites who never even went
down to Egypt and came back. They stayed in Palestine
and linked up again with their brethren on their return.

Individual attacks

Quite apart from the hints of previous occupation by
some of the Israelites, there are also clear statements
that individual groups made individual efforts in conquering and taking possession of the land. The attack of
Simeon and Judah in the South is quite independent of
Joshua (Jg 1:1-10, 17-19), though Caleb's attack on
Hebron (12-15), originally independent of Joshua, is
artificially brought into relation with him (Jos 14:6-15):
it is he who 'gives' Hebron to Caleb. But an indication
that Judah and Caleb were already installed is the
mention that Moses had long ago promised land to
Caleb. The scene suggests more a pact between Joshua
and already settled inhabitants of the land, who join
forces with the conquering invader. The whole of the
section in Joshua (13-19) describing the apportioning of
various territories to the tribes as the work of Joshua is
obviously a literary fiction. The author is describing the

boundaries of the tribes as he knew them in his own day, and invoking Joshua as the authority for them, since he is regarded as the prime mover in the land settlement. By ascribing the apportionment of the land of the tribes to God's instrument in the organisation of the land settlement (Jos 1:1-5) the author is expressing Yahweh's sanction for the situation of the chosen people.

The movement of the people of Israel into Palestine was not, then, so homogeneous as appears at first sight. It was a gradual penetration in various ways, spread over many centuries. The league of twelve tribes, united by their worship of Yahweh and their acceptance of the covenant with him on Sinai, existed fully only after the settlement of the Israelites in Palestine. For the previous history of the component elements in this league we have only fragmentary and unconnected information, chiefly concerned with central points of their faith, the promise to Abraham, the deliverance from Egypt, the covenant on Sinai (cf M. Noth, *Ueberlieferungs-geschichte des Pentateuch*, 1948, p 278). Many scholars would hold that these elements are not necessarily the history of the same group within what later became the league of twelve tribes, but that the continuous story is the result of the amalgamation of the histories of different groups within the league after they had pooled their fortunes and so their histories (eg Eissfeldt, *op cit*, p 15-17). Whether this is accepted or not, it remains clear that almost the sole link between the disparate units which made up the people of Israel in the promised land was their adherence to and dependence on Yahweh. The fragmentation evident from the Book of Judges, eg ch 5 — where most component tribes of the league are enumerated, and several censured for failure to come to help in the crisis — shows that already by this time Israel as a political entity was collapsing. This throws into still greater relief the strength of the religious ties.

Jericho

The story of the conquest of Palestine under Joshua, as told in Joshua 2-11, is then incomplete. But if chapters 2-10 give a historical account of the conquest by one tribe, Benjamin, we have at least a representative which the other conquests may resemble. In this particular case we can see back behind the literary stage of the book better than in most cases. The stories which form the basis of this part of the book are all popular stories of a well-defined type, stories which explain historically some curious feature which would be noticed by men of a later age. They would ask why such a good site as Jericho was deserted (it remained deserted well into the ninth century: 1 Kg 16:34); what was the origin of the acres of fallen stones, still striking today, called The Ruin (Ai) near Bethel; how the men of Gibeon came to have a relationship to the Israelites unique among the older inhabitants of Canaan; why the cave at Makkedah was blocked with great stones (10:27). All these were associated in the popular imagination with the great act of supernatural protection and power which was the entry into Canaan. Whether this association was correct or not is not of primary importance. What is of primary importance is the prominent place in the mind of the men of Benjamin shown by it: they were acutely conscious that their existence in this place and in these circumstances was due to arrangements made for their sake by Yahweh. There is, in fact, little reason to doubt the correctness of the association in some form or other, though no doubt the details were subsequently filled in; the great liturgical procession which ended in the capture of Jericho is somewhat too stylised to carry conviction; Rahab and her scarlet cord surely had originally a more important role than they retain in the bible. But a destruction of Jericho c 1325 is perfectly possible. Erosion has destroyed all evidence in the town itself, but the tombs nearby cease to be filled after that date, which suggests that the city was deserted. The case of Ai is more complicated and more interesting, for Ai was destroyed several centuries before the exodus, and not again inhabited till some centuries after the occupation of Canaan; it cannot then have been stormed and sacked as described in Jos 7:2-8:29. Some German scholars claim that the story is a mere invention to account for the gigantic ruins, others (cf J. Bright, *History of Israel*, 1960, p 119, following W. F. Albright) that the story of the sack of Bethel in the late thirteenth century has been transferred to Ai, a mere mile away. Such popular legends do easily come slightly adrift. There may well, then, be a genuine folk memory at the base of the particular stories of the settlement of the tribe of Benjamin.

The massacres

What, then, of the massacres? On various occasions in the story of the conquest it is recorded that the

Israelites massacred all the people of captured towns
(6:21; 8:24-9; 10:28-39; 11:14, 20). On one occasion
this is said to be done on the direct order of Yahweh
(8:2). Outside the Book of Joshua this wholesale
massacre occurs only in Num 31:14-18; Jg 21:11; in
both cases it is punishment for a specific offence. There
is also the case of Agag and the Amalekites (1 Sam 15:3,
33), where the massacre is regarded specifically as an act
of worship; this is the last time it occurs in action.

Various attempts have been made to explain this
barbarous practice. Some say it was a condition of the
survival of the purity of the Hebrew faith that the
inhabitants of the land should be massacred to avoid
contamination, pointing out that when primitive
peoples come into richer, sedentary and agricultural
civilisation they almost invariably adopt their gods and
forms of worship. This argument sounds dangerously
like 'the end justifies the means'. But in any case it was
not a condition of survival of the Hebrew faith, since for
centuries Israel lived cheek by jowl with the Canaanites
of Palestine. Others argue that the ban is largely a
theoretical measure, found above all in the artifical laws
of Deuteronomy, and in Joshua only as the result of a
much later editing. There is some measure of truth in
this; it fits into the idea of a mighty tidal-wave conquest
better than into the historical reality of a laborious and
heterogeneous advance. But Agag can hardly be disposed of in this way.

The ban was an integral part of the concept of a holy
war which Israel inherited from the neighbouring
peoples. This had definite rules and rites which made
the whole war a sacral act. The god was fighting for his
people and must receive his share of the spoils in

sacrifice (R. de Vaux, *Institutions de l'Ancien Testament* II, 1965, pp 73-7). For a time at any rate Israel, as might be expected, retained many of the values of her neighbours. It is only doubtful whether Israel had much opportunity of applying this particular rite. The only case where the details and circumstances indicate that such a slaughter actually took place is that of Agag. In the others mentioned it is passed over so casually that we may perhaps regard it as the interpretation of the final editor of the story; there are none of the circumstantial details which inspire confidence in the face-value historicity of a narrative. It is significant that, in the only other case of the ban which gains more than a passing mention (Jos 7:2-26), the interest centres on the violation of the ban by surreptitious filching of plunder — a story which rings very true; punishment is on the plunderer, and no massacre of the captives enters in. Agag, however, resists attempts to conjure him away as a product of later interpretations in the light of theoretical legislation. But on the other hand we must remember that, while in Israel there is no case of the application of the ban after Agag, in neighbouring Moab Israelite captives are still being slaughtered under the ban two centuries later (Pritchard, *op cit*, p 320). Yahweh took to himself a people which was primitive and barbaric — if the archaeology of Palestine shows anything it is the low level of material civilisation during these two centuries of turmoil — and educated it only gradually to a higher notion of himself and of conduct worthy of his people.

4

At the waters of Babylon

The shock to the people of God when they woke up to find themselves at the waters of Babylon was clearly traumatic. the horror of this moment may be partly gauged by their unwillingness to believe that it was true. When Jeremiah writes to assure the deportees that they had better settle down for a long stay, one of them indignantly writes a letter to *The Times* (or the ancient equivalent) demanding that he should be silenced (Jer 29:24-32). Back in Jerusalem they would still not believe how radical the destruction was to be: when Jeremiah acts the prophecy of a second deportation by going about with a yoke on his neck, a more comforting rival takes the yoke and breaks it, as a sign that foreign domination is about to end (Jer 28). Ezekiel, among the first exiles, employs a series of fantastic publicity stunts in the attempt to convince them that Jerusalem is really doomed: he builds a model of a besieged city, he publicly lives on all the foulness of the food obtainable in a siege, he acts out a deportation — anything to bring home to them that the first deportation they had themselves undergone was no flash in the pan but only a harbinger of more destruction. There was no hope now for Judah and Jerusalem.

The tragedy of the situation was that their refusal to give up hope sprang from faith, a faith in God's protection and in the destiny of Jerusalem and the

house of David. Any unbiased outside observer could
have told them that destruction and deportation were
inevitable. Even today the records of the successive
Mesopotamian empires of Assyria and Babylon can
re-create vividly the impression of a massive steam-roller
movement, the inexorable military machine crawling
progressively westwards to the Mediterranean and then
southwards towards Egypt, engulfing the little independent states which stood in the way. On the annual
records of campaigns appears the dreary repeated series
of events: first a state is raided and plundered, then it is
made tributary, soon it tries to shake off the yoke and is
finally crushed, losing its individuality and being swal-
lowed up in the amorphous mass of the empire by
deportation (*Ancient Near Eastern texts,* ed J.
Pritchard, 1955, pp 274-305). Judah had seen her
neighbours to the North disappear one by one,
Damascus, Galilee, Samaria itself. In the reign of
Sennacherib Judah had been devastated, but the power
of God to protect his people had been shown by the
unprecedented withdrawal of the army when Jerusalem
itself seemed in the grasp of the Assyrians (*ANET,* p
288: 2 Kg 18:13-19:37). Thus would the men of
Jerusalem and Judah have replied to the outside
observer who pointed to the lesson of recent history to
show the inevitable next step, that Jerusalem and the
people of God were different. They could not be
destroyed or deported because they had the promise of
protection from Yahweh; he was more powerful than
any other nation's god, and more intimately bound to
his people, with his presence in the temple of Jerusalem.
They thought that they need only repeat endlessly like a
charm: 'This is the sanctuary of Yahweh, this is the

sanctuary of Yahweh' (Jer 7:4) to ensure themselves
that this protection would never fail them, and when
Jeremiah drew to their attention the fate of the
sanctuary in the northern kingdom, where the presence
of Yahweh had once rested (7:12), the comparison cut
no ice. Their confidence in survival was a confidence in
Yahweh and his fidelity to his promises; this was what
made them so pathetic.

They needed the exile

This confidence was misplaced, for God's people had
partly forgotten and partly not yet realised what these
promises really were; it needed the cataclysm of the
exile for them to learn. What they had forgotten was
that they had been chosen to be God's people.
Associated with him they must follow his ways, and
show his name or nature to the world. The message of
the pre-exilic prophets, denouncing, cajoling, menacing,
was that there can be no protection from Yahweh
without fidelity in worship towards him alone, and
without social justice. The mere fact of having been
chosen as God's special people is no guarantee of
immunity: worse — it is a positive guarantee of
correction if Israel does not act like God's people. This
is part of the meaning of Hosea's image of Israel as the
bride of Yahweh. Once Israel has been betrothed to
Yahweh she cannot act like other nations, for association with Yahweh carries with it moral obligations.
Man and wife, two in one flesh, cannot be totally
disparate in character, but come closer and closer
together until they think and act with one mind.

Hosea's denunciation of Israel is that Israel does not show the qualities of Yahweh in her action, shows no knowledge of what Yahweh really is:

> There is no fidelity, no tenderness, no knowledge of God in the country, only perjury and lies, slaughter, theft. (Hos 4:2)

The purpose of the law had been to show what were the implications of being God's people, what the nature of Yahweh's bride must be. This began to be realised more and more clearly at the time of the exile. It is in the Book of Deuteronomy, published a mere twenty years before the fall of Jerusalem, that the principle becomes explicit that the Israelite must act towards others as God acted towards Israel. He must be generous to the poor as Yahweh had been generous in giving the land to Israel (Deut 15:7-11): in his conduct towards slaves he must remember that he is Yahweh's slave (15:15). During the exile itself this becomes clearer still. By intimate contact with a dominating nation, whose ways it would have been natural to follow, Israel became by contrast more conscious of its own individuality and separateness from other peoples; they were set apart, different from the world at large, just as Yahweh was wholly separate from and other than the world. This is the basic meaning of 'holiness'; in the circumstances of a captive people where the great danger was assimilation to the customs and ideas of the captors, the ensemble of the obligations on Israel which spring from her special relationship to Yahweh are therefore expressed in this way: 'Be holy, for I, Yahweh your God, am holy' (Lev 19:2).

It is this new sense of the need for his people to imitate God in their action which is expressed by Jeremiah's promise that 'They shall be my people and I shall be their God. I will give them a different heart and different behaviour' (Jer 32:38-9), or Ezekiel's (36:26), 'I shall remove the heart of stone from your bodies and give you a heart of flesh instead'. This heart will be a living heart, a centre of activity which is sensitive to the demands of God's law and to the needs of men, which will enable Israel no longer to be dead in the petrified conviction that they are the chosen people, but to live out this conviction in the awareness of its consequences of representing the love and fidelity of Yahweh towards men.

The lesson that God's choice is not a static privilege, given once and for all time, which may then be taken for granted, is the chief moral of the so-called Deuteronomic histories. With the example of the destruction of the northern kingdom and the dispersal of its people before their eyes, and with at least the threat of destruction hanging over Jerusalem (and the final edition at any rate was prepared when the exile had already begun), the scribes of Israel collected and composed the history of the people from Joshua to the end of the monarchy. Constantly recurring in these historical books is the reminder that not merely election but fidelity to God's commands is what gains his favour and protection (eg Jos 1:6-9; 23:6-11; Jg 2:11-23, etc). When Israel is faithful to Yahweh it enjoys prosperity; when it deserts his paths he brings it back by corrective punishment until it turns to him again. This is the moral which the historians saw in the history of Israel, and pointed out by recurring editorial comment.

True destiny discovered

More important even than this recall to the way in which they must live out their vocation was the deepening of Israel's understanding of its ultimate vocation which was wrought by the exile.

It would be difficult to date the start of Israel's awareness that she had a special destiny, as opposed to the more pedestrian conviction that Yahweh, her own god, would protect her as other nations were protected by other gods — except of course that Yahweh was more powerful than any other god, and therefore his protection would not fail. A definite step forward in the explicitness of this hope in some everlasting destiny is taken at the time of David, when Nathan prophesies to him (2 Sam 7) that his line will be eternal, and his throne established for ever. But the conviction of the destiny of Israel to which this prophecy gave rise — and it is constantly echoed in psalms and other literature thenceforth — was still narrowly nationalistic: Israel's destiny concerned only herself, there was no idea of any mission or benefit to other nations; and the everlasting rule of the dynasty of David was conceived as being on the same level as the rule of other dynasties, only longer and perhaps more glorious. It seems to us now that this primitive messianism (for so one may call it) was in this undeveloped state self-centred and largely materialistic.

In the great royal psalms the poetic language is hard to evaluate, and indeed being poetry is not intended to be exactly evaluated. To some it seems that the extravagant promises of Ps 2 must imply rule over something different in kind, not merely larger and more invincible, than the little kingdom of Judah: 'You are

my son . . . ask and I will give you the nations for your
heritage, the ends of the earth for your domain.' Even
more portentous — whatever the details of its corrupt
text — is Ps 110. Here there must be at least an
undefined intuition that the king to whom it was
applied in the first instance stood in a line whose
destiny transcended the narrow limits of earthly
kingship. This development continues in the messianic
prophecies of Isaiah, where there is a realisation not
only that the king in whom the line is to culminate will
be at least in some way more than earthly, 'Wonder-
Counsellor, Mighty God, Eternal Father, Prince of
Peace' (9:6), but also that the state of the kingdom over
which he rules will be one of a peace and justice not
known in the present dispensation (7:21-5; 9:7; 11:3-9).
But the progression to the realisation of this goal is still
conceived as rectilinear. It is a development and
flowering of the Davidic kingship as it then existed in
Judah.

The radically new dimension introduced into the
messianic hope by the exile was a sense of failure. With
the total collapse of the monarchy, of the temple, of all
institutions and everything which Israel valued, the rosy
confidence in the condition of Israel, and indeed of the
world in general, vanished. There came the awareness of
guilt and sin which is so marked a characteristic of
post-exilic biblical literature (the *Miserere*; Bar 1:1-3:8):
perhaps even the narrative of the fall reached its final
form at this period. The consequence of this sense of
failure and of the destruction of the national and
religious institutions was the realisation that the ideal
world longed for and expected was not the natural
outcome of the present state of affairs; it required a

fundamental upheaval. Firstly there must be a purging away of evil, whose proportions were realised only by the reflection on the continual failure of Israel. Hence the powerful metaphors of the prophets: two baskets of figs, one good and one rotten (Jer 24), the felled stump of Jesse from which a new shoot will spring (Is 11:1), purging by fire like silver until all the base metal is burnt away (Is 1:25; 48:10). Only a remnant of Israel would remain, but a remnant tested and purified by suffering; God's punishment had a purpose, not only the removal of the dross of old Israel but the preparation of a new and finer stem.

Rebirth

This, however, was only the negative aspect; more important was the realisation that what amounted to a new creation was needed in order to achieve the ideal messianic state of affairs prophesied, eg by Isaiah. The messiah himself, the ideal king, goes right into the background, instead of being (as before the exile) the backbone of all hope for the future. He is still there, in the background, since part of the promise for the future is a new David, representative of God, who will pasture God's sheep in the new pasture-lands (Ez 34:23). It is the rebirth of the whole of Israel which holds the centre of the stage. The prophets searched for symbols under which to describe this resurgence and radical newness. It could, of course, be described only in terms of or in comparison to the past and, further, Israel had by now firmly fixed the image of an ideal state of affairs at the dawn of time, a paradise, before evil was introduced into the world. But that it was represented as a return need not prevent us, with our minds formed in the perspective of Newman, Darwin and Teilhard de Chardin, seeing it less in terms of a return to an ideal past than in terms of advance to a state which has never yet existed but remains the ideal intended from the first by God.

The images used by the prophets to express this renewal are various, different models each pointing to a different aspect of the reality. Jeremiah uses the idea of a new covenant, echo of the covenant which brought Israel into being as God's people, and remained the guarantee of his love (Jer 31:31-4). Ezekiel returns to the scene of the original creation of man when God 'breathed into his nostrils a breath of life and man became a living being' (Gen 2:7); Ezekiel takes up this imagery for his scene in the valley of dry bones, when the spirit (? Spirit) of God again gives life to the bones of the house of Israel (37:1-14). A disciple of Isaiah develops Isaiah's theme of paradisiac peace, 'the wolf and the young lamb will feed together' (Is 65:25, as 11:6); but the change which has taken place from the perspective of Isaiah himself is evident, in that all this involves a radical newness: 'Now I create a new heaven and a new earth, and the past will not be remembered'.

With the destruction of Jerusalem, then, the whole of Israel's hope and conception of its destiny moves into a new key. Before the exile Israel had the ambition of a rectilinear development of its power, centred upon the kingship of the line of David, involving limitless nationalistic dominion, leavened by barely a hint of transcendent peace. When this collapses there is room for a far broader vision; due place is given to failure, corruption and national incapacity, and the destiny of Israel is seen to be to provide the focus for a cosmic renewal by which these are overcome. What form this cosmic renewal will take is not yet clearly seen, but the shock of exile has begun to bear fruit.

5

The presence of God in the poverty of man

It is difficult not to regard the prophets of the last period of biblical history, the time of the return from the exile, as incorrigible dreamers. The nation had already been crushed, but its prophets had foretold a rebirth with a new heart and a new spirit. But when they returned to the holy land it was to failure and frustration of their ecstatic hopes. By reaction, or so it seems, these hopes, far from fading away, merely became more extreme and all-embracing. In an age of material prosperity and progress this would perhaps be explicable, but at a time of poverty, oppression and insignificance, of spiritual low temperature and indifference, it is a final proof of the resilient faith of a few.

Hardly had the disaster of the destruction and final deportation from Jerusalem occurred when the prophets Jeremiah and Ezekiel foretold that from the wreckage a remnant would be salvaged which would live with a new heart and a new spirit. Within thirty years there seemed some hope of liberation from captivity at Babylon, or at least a change of overlord, for Cyrus the Mede was gaining power on the frontier of the empire with such speed that a clash may well have seemed inevitable. So strong was the hope of the exiles that his appearance was greeted in rapturous terms by the unknown successor of Isaiah whom we now name Deutero-Isaiah. He calls Cyrus the Lord's anointed (45:1), blandly claiming that he had been appointed to sweep all before him for the specific purpose of setting Israel free. The return of the exiles is foretold in terms which deliberately compare it to the exodus from Egypt: Yahweh was claiming back his people for himself and would lead them through the desert to the accompaniment of the portents which had marked the journey from Egypt (41:18; 43:2, etc). But more than this: the prophet is filled with the sense of God's unbounded power as creator over the entire universe. For it is by contrast to the idols of the Babylonians (46:1-13) that the cosmic extent of God's power is first clearly perceived and praised. As creator he will not only renew the wonders of the exodus journey, but create a new paradise as he leads his people across the desert.

> I will make rivers well up on barren heights,
> and fountains in the midst of valleys;
> turn the wilderness into a lake
> and dry ground into waterspring.
> In the wilderness I will put cedar trees,
> acacias, myrtles, olives . . . (41:18-19)

Such was to be the new world envisaged by the prophet as inaugurated by Cyrus' approaching conquest of Babylon and — in accordance with his unexpectedly modern theories of controlling a large empire through the goodwill rather than the fear of his subjects — decree that the exiles of the Jews among others should be sent home, allowed to rebuild their temple, and that at his own expense (Ezr 6:3-5). It was, however, the

Jews themselves who failed to play the role cast for them. The response to the appeal to return to Judah was disappointing; many families had already settled down in their exile to become prosperous merchants and bankers, as the records show, and were no less reluctant than many modern Jews to exchange their comfortable situation for a precarious, though adventurous, existence on their ancestral soil. The list of those who actually returned (Ezr 2) is meagre, and even the tiny circuit of the walls rebuilt half a century later at Jerusalem was too big to be adequately repopulated (Neh 7:4). When they got there they were met by opposition at every stage, opposition from their neighbours the Samaritans (Ezr 4:5), from the governor of the province (4:6-23), from the local native magnates (Neh 4:1-2; 6:1-2, etc).

The result was, not surprisingly, acute discouragement. Some twenty years passed before the building of the temple actually got under way, and then only due to the constant badgering of the prophets Haggai and Zechariah. A series of bad harvests was not unconnected with this lassitude. Haggai attributes the bad harvests to failure to rebuild the temple (1:9-11; 2:15-19); no doubt both were partly symptoms of the same discouragement and listlessness. Once again, it seems, the chosen people had misunderstood the prophecies made to them, taking them in too material a sense. As before the exile they had taken God's promises as an infallible guarantee of the institutions of Israel, temple and monarchy, so now they had expected Judah to be a paradise on earth, in immediate and literal fulfilment of the prophecies of Deutero-Isaiah. Yet another purification was necessary. This further purification and refinement of the Jewish hope took place by two developments which — paradoxically — complement each other.

The poverty of man

The first is the appreciation of poverty, forced on them by their situation, as a precondition for service of Yahweh. In pre-exilic days material prosperity had been popularly regarded as the criterion of God's approval. This mentality persists in the proverbs of the wisdom literature (which in general often strikes us by its appearance of worldliness). The poor get little sympathy, for poverty is assumed to be the result of idleness:

> Pleasure-lovers stay poor,
> he will not grow rich who loves wine and good living.
> (Prov 21:17)

> The lips of a virtuous man nourish a multitude,
> but fools die in poverty. (10:21)

These sentiments are true enough, but there is a certain hardness and complacency about them which could not survive the changed circumstances of the return from exile. Now material prosperity must be finally and radically abandoned as a standard of godliness. Whatever prosperity had been built up in Judah by trade and agriculture during the period of the monarchy had vanished with the exile, and Palestine is a country whose fruitfulness declines sharply as soon as attention is

distracted from the laborious attempts to harbour its
scanty natural resources by irrigation, terracing of the
soil, etc. One can imagine the returning settlers reduced
to the condition of the wretched Arab peasants eking
out a living from the soil of Palestine before Western
technique and capital were applied to rehabilitate it.
This subsistence-level survival taught them its lesson,
until the ideal of acceptability with God became
entirely divorced from that of national or individual
prosperity. The conversion required for this to occur is
staggering. In an established bourgeois christianity it has
often proved almost impossible to avoid the tacit
assumption that at least corporate and national success
are criteria of divine favour — in spite of the beatitudes.
But when the attitude which was the seed-bed of the
beatitudes was being forged there was in addition the
background of the age-old assumption that prosperity
was the natural sign of God's favour. In spite of this,
one of the last representatives of the tradition of Isaiah
can announce his vocation in the words which Luke
later quoted to sum up Jesus' mission:

> Yahweh has anointed me.
> He has sent me to bring good news to the poor,
> to bind up hearts that are broken. (Is 61:1)

In the psalms, whose composition dates so largely from
these centuries, the ideal of destitution as the precondition for openness to the reception of God's help and
favour receives its fullest expression, to such an extent
that the cry of persecution becomes almost monoton-
ous. But in those days of poverty and oppression it had
a pressing reality which can escape us, which blossomed

in the realisation at last that if Israel was still God's people it was not for anything which Israel itself could offer but simply as willing to receive God's help and mercy.

The presence of God

To complement this attitude of humble receptiveness there took place a development in Israel's hope, a boundless enlargement of horizon. Before the exile Israel had looked for God's promises to be realised in the domination of his people over their neighbours; this hope was annihilated by the destruction of Israel as a nation. As the exile drew to a close there arose, as we have seen, an expectation of a return to an earthly paradise; but the actual circumstances of the return showed that this hope too must be radically reinterpreted. The reinterpretation took two different forms in different traditions. In the prophetic tradition the hope remained centred on Jerusalem but, directly in proportion as the likelihood of any material success or distinction became less, just so much did the assertions of the prophets grow stronger that

> In the days to come
> the mountain of the temple of Yahweh
> shall tower above the mountains.
> All the nations will stream to it,
> peoples without number will come to it. (Is 2:2-3)

In Isaiah's own prophecies this is an isolated saying, but in the tradition which he initiated the theme takes on

central importance precisely at the period of disappoint-
ment after the return from exile. During the exile it
does indeed reappear, in the form of a promise that
remote nations will express their submission to Yahweh
by submitting to Israel (Is 45:14-15; 49:23). But in the
last prophecies of the book of Isaiah the number of
these promises increases and their character changes.
There is no longer talk of 'submission'; now it is of
'recognition' of the greatness of God in Jerusalem, a
glad and willing acknowledgement:

> Nations come to your light
> and kings to your dawning brightness. (60:2-3)

> The nations then will see your integrity
> all the kings your glory. (62:2)

No longer has Israel anything to offer; the recognition
of all nations is purely for the God who makes
Jerusalem the dwelling-place of his glory:

> Hoist the signal for the peoples
> Say to the daughter of Zion, 'Look
> your saviour comes'. (62:11)

And this presence of Yahweh is recognised for its
integrity, for its peace (66:12; 26:3), because through
his presence in Jerusalem Yahweh will abolish death
(25:7). This is altogether a more lofty sort of leadership
than the military despotism formerly envisaged, an
immediate preparation for the kingdom of heaven which
Jesus was to proclaim.

Besides this Jerusalem-centred tradition another

development took place, even more ambitious in appearance, the apocalyptic movement. Starting from the conception of the Day of the Lord — used by the earlier prophets to predict the day of God's judgement on the shortcomings of Israel — it concentrates on the coming of the Lord amid awesome cosmic phenomena, now no longer so much to punish (though this aspect is still present) as to save and to renew the world. The cosmic imagery is splendid and fantastic:

> Oh, that you would tear the heavens
> open and come down.
> At your presence the mountains would melt
> as fire sets brushwood alight
> as fire causes water to boil. (Is 64:1-2)

But the emphasis is consistently on renewal: 'For now I create new heavens and a new earth' (65:17). It is as though the authors are groping, trying to express what cannot be put into words. It is conveyed partly by removal of all material ill: no more frost, no more darkness, unquenchable plenty of water in that arid land (Zech 14:6-8), no more weeping or devastation, no premature death or strife (Is 65:19-23). The Jews were not, however, naive enough to think that this renewal was simply a matter of the removal of physical unpleasantness; disharmony in nature is connected with, and was treated as the expression of, a deeper disharmony. Nor can it be adequately described as a moral renewal or regeneration; these are cold terms, and far too anthropocentric. Evil is indeed to be removed, as Zechariah saw in his vision (5:5-9), but this is a negative aspect. The positive side is expressed by the ever-repeated promises of the presence of God:

> I am coming back to Zion and shall dwell in the
> middle of Jerusalem. (Zech 8:3)

And this has as its consequence that everything is to be
made sacred, shot through with the effect of God's
presence:

> When that day comes, the horse-bells will be inscribed
> with the words 'Sacred to Yahweh' (Zech 14:20)

So in the last centuries before Christ God prepared his
people by the bitter disappointments of the return from
exile, finally weaning it from self-important ideas of
world domination, forming a poor and humble community which yet was sustained by the promise that
somehow through it God would transform the world by
his presence.

6

The childhood of Jesus

It has long been accepted that the gospel stories about the childhood of Jesus show considerable differences of treatment and tone from the rest of the gospels. Perhaps the most striking differences are the frequency with which angels appear and with which wonders occur. While in the rest of the gospels angels appear only twice altogether, after the temptations in the desert and at the empty tomb, in Matthew's infancy narrative alone an angel appears three times, and similarly in Luke's account. Further, on the two occasions in the rest of the gospel when they do appear they play no crucial role, whereas here they are central to the whole action. It is this which gives the action its atmosphere of the wonderful, a world in which human motivation is over-ridden by divine force. Another significant difference lies in the literary form: the rest of the gospel is formed of circumstantial stories which centre upon some action or word of Jesus preserved in the christian communities and originally vividly described in a self-contained little vignette — one thinks of the controversies with the pharisees or the healing of the epileptic boy. But in the infancy narratives the stories do not seem to have kernels of the kind which formed the nucleus of the stories of the gospel tradition in the earliest gospel, Mark. Indeed the Acts of the Apostles makes it clear that the earliest preaching began, as do the gospels of Mark and John, with the baptism of

Jesus; one might therefore legitimately expect the stories of Jesus' earlier life to be of a different stamp. It is a recognised phenomenon of popular literature — and it is in this class that the gospels fall — that stories about the childhood of a hero begin to be told later than the stories about his time of greatness; obviously people must have their attention attracted by his achievements before they begin to ask about his boyhood. This does not, of course, say that the stories of his boyhood are false, but only shows that they are likely to have been composed from a different angle, and with more developed and mature thought about the hero.

Folk tales?

In the stories about Jesus' boyhood told by Matthew the situation is complicated because there are definite themes of folk-literature to be found. The second chapter revolves round figures well known in such literature, a wicked king and oriental magicians, whose presence contrasts markedly with the atmosphere of countryside, peasants and fishermen which characterises the rest of the gospel story. More particularly, the theme of the wicked old king who is told of the birth of a destined rival and tries to kill the baby, who in his turn is saved through superhuman protection, is a familiar one: Oedipus and Romulus and Remus spring to mind. The appearance of a star at the birth of a great man is similarly a frequent motif, especially at this era: it is told of King Nimrud, of Augustus and Nero, and soon becomes a commonplace.

Once it has been observed that these stories show

certain similarities with folk-tales the question is raised of the sense in which they are to be regarded as true. Are they true only in the sense in which *The Lord of the Rings* or C. S. Lewis' fairy stories are true? X. Léon-Dufour, in *The Gospels and the History of Jesus* (1968), pp 214-18, continues the standard catholic practice of accepting them as true unless they can be proved to be false, and thus regarding their similarity to folk-literature as purely coincidental. There is a certain narrowness about each of these attitudes, which generates the sort of frustration produced when a reader refuses to take a document in the sense in which it was written. Certainly it would not be easy to prove that the stories were false: oriental wizards and magic were rampant in Palestine at this time; Herod was a bloodthirsty tyrant, whose insane fear of rivals induced him to execute several relatives in his later years, and would have led him to kill off without scruple the mere handful of boys born during two years in a tiny hamlet of the hill-country. Attempts to interpret the star as a description of various astronomical phenomena known to have occurred just before the turn of the eras have not wholly succeeded, for nothing can account for the fact that the star moves and then stands still over Bethlehem; this double phenomenon does not fit any of the suggested stars or comets. Nevertheless it could seem reasonable to claim that the improbabilities are thereby reduced to a mere poetical adjustment.

But the discovery that the stories are close to those current in folklore casts a new light on the enquiry. It cannot be legitimate simply to disregard this fact, especially in view of the striking differences already mentioned between these stories and the rest of the gospel. A comparison should surely be made with similar folk themes found in other stories about the infancy of great men to determine, not primarily their historical exactitude, but the way in which the story-teller meant them. It cannot be assumed that the author intended his reader to believe that he was relating historical events for their own sake. He is interested primarily not in the events themselves which he is describing but in the person whose quality they show. Thus, when ancient authors tell of St Ambrose and various other great preachers that a swarm of bees or a honeycomb was found in the infants' mouths, the prime purpose is to show that the infants were destined to be 'honey-tongued'; one would show a wholly wrong attitude if one asked the date on which this occurred. Similarly when a foundling child, destined to greatness, is suckled by a wolf or other animal, one should not ask to be told the place where this happened but should understand the story as an indication of supernatural preservation and protection for the sake of the destiny which awaits him. Different canons of verification apply to different kinds of literature: in the two cases just mentioned a convincing refutation would consist not in a minute-to-minute analysis of the subject's childhood, but in a demonstration respectively that he was not a great preacher and that he achieved no great destiny to which he could have been preserved by the gods.

The case for understanding Matthew's stories in this way — as lessons about the person of Jesus but not necessarily about the historical events of his early life — would be immensely strengthened if parallels could be quoted for the biblical text. These can in fact be found, and in two ways, both large-scale embroidering of basic data (which can be found in the Jewish tradition, of which the case of Moses is soon to be mentioned) and in Matthew's own tendency to alter unimportant factual details in his source in order to bring out more clearly the meaning of the event as a whole, and so throw a more complete light on the person of Jesus, or for other reasons. Thus in 27:34 Matthew is certainly following Mark's account, but he changes Mark's 'they offered him wine mixed with myrrh' into 'wine mixed with gall'; one of his dominant interests is to show how minutely Jesus fulfilled the will of the Father as expressed in scripture, and this he does here by working in a fulfilment of Ps 68:21: 'they gave me gall for food' (cf p 96). On another occasion, where Mark (10:46) tells of a blind man cured at Jericho, Matthew (20:30), following Jewish law requiring two witnesses, makes it two blind men. A number of such minor adjustments show that Matthew does not have the meticulous concern for factual exactitude which a modern historian would claim, but is quite content with the broader fidelity of the *raconteur*.

To pass to the subject of folk-motifs and larger-scale embroidery, there is at least one other instance in Matthew where such a motif is surely to be seen. This is the case of the coin found in the fish's mouth (17:27), a theme which occurs both in Greek literature (Polycrates' ring is familiar) and in rabbinic stories, where there are several instances of men of God proving their authority by finding jewels in the mouth of a fish. In view of this it is hard to deny that in this incidental flourish at the end of a story, the biblical author is probably drawing on a stock theme rather than on historical memory. The introduction of such motifs was

not, then, alien to the evangelists as a way of showing
the significance of Jesus. Nor would one expect it to be,
for such techniques were the current coin of Jewish
religious literature at the time at which they wrote. An
excellent example of the way these techniques were
used is provided by the stories about the boyhood of
Moses current in the first century: the biblical story
provides a basis, but details are filled out and wonders
multiplied. This example is particularly useful to the
present discussion because there are unmistakable con-
nections between these stories and the second chapter
of Matthew.

Moses and Jesus

The story in the Book of Exodus is well known;
significant elements are added to it by the legends.
Moses' father was warned in a dream of the king's plan
to do away with the child, so that he could save him.
The king is warned supernaturally that this great figure
has been born among the Hebrews: he and all his court
are thrown into confusion by the news, and he consults
his magicians, who interpret the omens to him. Thus the
atmosphere of the marvellous is heightened and the
important destiny and divine protection of Moses
brought out more clearly; the means used to do this are
the common elements of the folk tale of the wicked
king and the destined supplanter. The story continues,
but the parallel with Matthew's story has already been
established: in each case the jealous king thrown into
confusion by the news of the birth of a possible rival; in
each case he calls his advisers together; in each case the

magicians interpret to him — only in Matthew the magicians are not his own henchmen but are contrasted with him: the reverence for God's word and the acceptance of God's promises shown by these gentiles serve to underline the stubborn refusal of the Jews to whom the word and the promises were primarily addressed. In each case the king then attempts unsuccessfully to eliminate the young boy. Before the last scene of Matthew's drama, the return to the homeland from Egypt, a considerable time-lapse intervenes; in the case of Moses this was even longer, for the parallel to this scene is the return of Moses from Midian, where he only took refuge when already a grown man. But the comparison is made unmistakable, despite the reversal of movement (Moses' homeland was Egypt, so it is *to* Egypt that he returns; Jesus: homeland was Palestine, so it is thither that he returns *from* Egypt), by Matthew giving even a verbal parallel in 2:20 to Ex 4:19.

This elaborate parallel between the boyhoods of Moses and of Jesus is, then, no coincidence; but what is its purpose? The expectation that the Messiah was to be a second Moses was extremely prominent in Jewish thought at the time of Christ. It was founded on the promise to Moses in Deut 18:15: 'Yahweh your God will raise up for you a prophet like myself . . . to him you must listen.' The echo of the last phrase in the narrative of the transfiguration (Mt 17:5) is obvious. The claim to be a second Moses is frequently implicit in the claims of the false messiahs mentioned by Josephus. In the riot whose mishandling led to Pilate's dismissal from the office of prefect of Judaea, the centre of attraction was a promise to lead the crowd to the sacred vessels buried by Moses. The thought behind this is the

conviction, amply attested also by the rabbinic evidence, that redemption by the messiah will repeat the
liberation from Egypt under Moses' leadership. In
Matthew the theme reappears, but here the main point
of the parallel is with Moses the legislator: as Moses gave
the law on Mount Sinai, so Jesus gives the new law in
the sermon on the mount, perfecting the Mosaic law.
The parallel is also clear in the story of Jesus'
temptations in the desert. The whole story is told in
such a way as to recall the testing of Israel during forty
years in the desert, but the parallel with Moses is
especially stressed by Matthew: Jesus fasts for forty
days and forty nights in preparation, as did Moses (Deut
9:9); finally, as Moses at the end of his life saw all the
promised land from the top of a mountain, so Jesus sees
all the kingdoms of the earth.

In the stories of the flight into Egypt and the return
Matthew is doing no more than extend into Jesus'
childhood this comparison to Moses, showing that
already Jesus was the prophet like Moses who was to
come. The chief language available to the evangelists for
showing the significance of the person of Jesus was that
drawn from the old testament. Particularly in Matthew's
community, which we may deduce remained closer to
semitic judaism than those in which the other gospels
were written, the interpretation of Jesus in terms of a
second Moses, who renewed and completed the work
done by the first Moses, would have been meaningful
and inspiring. Their religious thoughts and images were
built on the old testament, and it was inevitably to this
source that they returned to seek understanding of
Jesus, in much the same way as the puritans returned to
the bible to seek understanding (or at least expression of

it) of the events and figures of their own time. Thus it is in the old testament terms of Elijah or 'the prophet' that the envoys from Jerusalem try to explain John the Baptist, and in the words of Isaiah that he offers his own explanation (Jn 1:19-23). At Caesarea Philippi the disciples quote the opinions that Jesus is 'Elijah, Jeremiah or one of the prophets' (Mk 8:29); and even Peter's final acknowledgement, 'the Christ', is similarly an old testament term, packed with overtones and nuances for one familiar with the prophets and largely devoid of them for one who is not: full of significance therefore to a Jew and almost meaningless to a gentile.

The story of Jesus' childhood told by Matthew raises, then, in an acute form the problem of the modern man's understanding of the new testament and particularly of the gospels. They were written in a certain set of circumstances and against a certain literary and religious background, where a word or an image could be sufficient to evoke a whole world of ideas. Most of us have now lost this background (and may even be unaware of the fact of its existence). Therefore when Matthew describes Jesus to us in terms of Moses we have not normally sufficient shared experience to appreciate what these terms mean to him, what warmth and depth they conjure up. To the Jew Moses was, under God, the founder of the chosen people, the chosen servant of God who led God's people into the freedom of loving intimacy with Yahweh, the instrument of God picked out and formed to mediate his eternal law to them, to give fixed form to all that was most sacred. There was no greater figure in world history to whom Jesus could be compared, for he had given the definitive structure and norms which were to last for all time to come until the coming of the figure who was to renew and complete his work. If we cannot appreciate, intellectually and emotionally, the meaning of the Moses-figure at the time of the evangelists, we are like one who tries to understand remarks made about the moon in the 1970s from the standpoint of the 1870s. One might say that from being a symbol of romance the moon has been transformed into the symbol of man's belief in his ability to achieve all things by technology, the spearhead of his hope. It conjures up images not of languorous lovers but of purposeful, ungainly creatures thrusting forward in the conquest of the unknown. It was because already Byzantine christianity had lost the sense of the old testament that they took pains to identify the tree at Heliopolis in Egypt (still shown to the intrepid traveller) under which the holy family sat. Long before that again the 'infancy gospel' of the second century had set a wrong course. Such failure to appreciate the author's meaning was inevitable, as soon as christianity was torn away from its semitic roots. To what extent can the damage be repaired? To what extent should repair work be attempted?

7

The adoption of Jesus

The virginity of Mary has always been one of the most warmly asserted doctrines of the catholic tradition in the church. According to Origen there was early current a gibe that Jesus was in fact the son of a Roman soldier (*Contra Celsum* 1:26) — an assertion that the church has always hotly denied. But the importance of this doctrine and the heat it has generated have tended to make believers see it as central in scriptural passages where it is no more than peripheral. The common attitude to the first story in Matthew's gospel has been largely determined by this apologetic preoccupation: when the angel appears to Joseph his purpose has commonly been taken to be to defend Mary's virginity, and the other data of the story have been quite eclipsed by the attention paid to the passing remark 'he had not had intercourse with her when . . .' (1:25). The main purpose of the story is, however, quite different.

In the previous chapter it was contended that the main drive of Matthew's second chapter was not to give information about the infancy of Jesus but to explain his person by showing that he is the second Moses, the ultimate prophet whose stature can be described only in function of that towering figure who established the order by which the life of the chosen people had been determined. Now in the same way the first chapter seeks to explain the person of Jesus in terms of another

towering figure of the Jewish messianic hope, David.
Jesus himself had been at best reserved about applying
to himself the title 'Son of David'; many exegetes
maintain that he rejected it altogether, although it is so
prominent in the old testament prophecies (eg Ez 36).
The only saying of his reported by Mark in which he
uses the title (the question in the temple, Mk 12:35-7)
at least points out that the ascription of the title to the
messiah involves difficulties. Some would say that Jesus
is hinting that it is altogether inappropriate, though it is
perhaps more consonant with Jesus' pedagogy that he
should be inciting them to reflection on the implications
of the verse of Ps 110. Be that as it may, in Matthew,
writing as he was for an audience for whom the old
testament prophecies of Christ were of supreme importance, the title 'Son of David' takes on a far greater role.
Whereas in Mark Jesus is called by this title only once
(10:47-8), in Matthew it becomes a fairly regular
designation for him by the crowds: the blind man of
9:27, the enthusiastic crowds of 12:23, the Canaanite
woman of 15:22, and the acclaiming throngs at the
entry to Jerusalem (21:9, 15). In at least the second and
fourth of these cases it seems to be used in a special
sense, much as we would use 'Christ' itself, which was
originally a descriptive term and has become a proper
name.

It was, then, of considerable significance to Matthew
and to his readers that Jesus was the Son of David, the
promised scion of the line of the priest-king who was so
idealised in Jewish tradition, whose son and successor
was to restore Israel. In this way it was possible to show
from the start who Jesus was. The only difficulty was
that Jesus was not, according to the most straight-

forward reckoning and certainly according to our way of thinking, a descendant of David. This has so worried generations of believers that a sort of understanding has grown up in the church that Mary was of the line of David (hence the curious custom of reading Joseph's genealogy on the feast of the birthday of our Lady — they are presumed to be pretty well the same). But there is nothing at all in scripture to suggest that this was the case. One might even argue in the opposite direction, that she was of levitic stock because her cousins Zechariah and Elizabeth were (Lk 1:5). Further, at least in rabbinic times (Strack-Billerbeck 1, 5), descent through the female line was considered less honourable than through the male line; the same is surely implied for the time of the evangelists also by the exclusively male character of both Matthew's and Luke's genealogies. But if Jesus had no human father, how was his title of descent from David to be established? The solution provided by adoption was far stronger then than it is today, when we cannot really bring ourselves to acknowledge an adopted son as fully the son of his adoptive father (perhaps through greater knowledge of the determining influence of heredity). There was at least one important case provided for by the law where mere physical paternity did not decide a child's real paternity: by the law of the levirate if a man died without a son, his brother must beget a son and heir to the dead man on the dead man's wife (cf Mk 12:19); this cannot have been all that rare, and so the possibilty of real but not physical sonship would have been a present reality to the Jews.

The way in which a father acknowledged a son as his own was by naming him. Thus when Joseph names Jesus

he is accepting him as his son: it is no wonder that the
people of Nazareth thought that Jesus was 'the son of
the craftsman'. (Matthew's version, 13:55; Mark's more
original text makes Jesus the craftsman and has no
mention of his father; thus we see Matthew's preoccupation with descent from David in this piece of
editing also.) And they were right too, for Jesus was the
son of Joseph, even without the physical act of
generation. This is the reason for the prominence
accorded to Joseph in this passage and this passage
alone. Luke, less interested in the Davidic descent of
Jesus, gives the message of the divine conception of
Jesus much more straightforwardly by his narrative of
the message of the angel to Mary. This is not only more
direct than a message to Joseph about Mary. Both
Matthew's and Luke's narratives are in some measure
modelled upon the story of the annunciation of the
birth of Samson to his mother (Jg 13). But there the
announcement comes to the mother and the naming is
done by the mother; in Matthew it is the father, Joseph.
Matthew is, therefore, unnecessarily tortuous and un-
faithful to his original unless he is deliberately and
forcefully making these changes for a special purpose:
because Joseph must be brought into prominence,
Joseph must accept the child as his own.

As Matthew rightly saw, however, there were still two
difficulties: it is curious that Joseph should calmly
acknowledge as his own a child who is not, physically,
his own, especially if he knows the true origin of the
child; such bland effrontery would take a lot of beating.
Secondly, it is not enough that Jesus should be son of
David thanks to a mere chance whim of man; it must be
by the 'will of God himself'. This is the function of the

angel. For Joseph is duly hesitant and intends not to complete his marriage with Mary, until the angel removes this hesitation. But it must be noted that the only positive command which the angel gives, at the very centre of the passage (the name 'Jesus' occurs three times, at beginning, centre and end, verses 18, 21, 25), is that Joseph should name him, ie take the child for his own. The climax of the passage duly comes at the end, when Joseph performs this. This first story should not, then, be entitled, as it so often is, 'The birth of Christ' or even 'The virginal conception of Jesus'. The point is the naming and consequent adoption of Jesus into the house of David. If it is regarded in this way the genealogy of Joseph, his descent from David and before that from Abraham, the ultimate father of the chosen people, is no longer an independent list, curiously ending with the husband of Jesus's mother, but falls perfectly into place as the genealogy of Joseph, scion of the house of David and father of Jesus, and of Jesus himself, the Son of David.

The crucial question which demands discussion in the above interpretation is why Joseph needed the intervention of a special message from God to induce him to take Mary to himself, why he was intending to put her away. The common view, ruled by the stress on Mary's virginity, is that he suspected her of adultery. For although the marriage had not yet been completed by Mary's moving into Joseph's house, sexual misconduct after the betrothal (much more final than a modern 'engagement') ranked as adultery. The message from God then comes to guarantee to him, and to us, her innocence and the supernatural origin of the child. There are, however, a number of difficulties about this view. In a class by itself ranks the human or psychological difficulty that this interpretation presupposes an extraordinary lack of confidence between the betrothed pair: either Mary did not tell him how she was pregnant or he did not believe her. Despite the picture of the comic and doltish old man by which mediaeval legends represent Joseph, he was presumably, like Mary, in his early teens and would surely know enough of his betrothed and her radiant and pure simplicity to recognise that adultery would have been totally out of character. On these grounds alone it seems extraordinary that christians should have maintained that the purpose of the message was to allay his suspicions.

'A just man'

This conclusion is supported by strictly exegetical considerations. Joseph is called, precisely in this connexion, 'a just man'. The force of the adjective cannot be weakened to, eg, the Jerusalem Bible's 'a man of honour', for Matthew of all the evangelists is most concerned with the Jewish law, and especially in this Jewish context it must mean 'law-abiding', cf 23:28. P. Spicq (RB 71, 1964, pp 206-14) suggests that *dikaios* here means 'generous, merciful, magnanimous' — 'the just is purely and simply the perfect man' (p 208). But it is perhaps in order to suggest that P. Spicq is here misled rather than enlightened by his incomparable knowledge of contemporary extra-biblical Jewish literature; for Josephus and Philo use the word not in its strict Jewish sense but in a related sense which would be intelligible and acceptable as an ideal to their hellenistic readers. The reason why this is important is that the penalty for adultery was stoning, and Joseph could in no sense be called 'law-abiding' if he had attempted to shield his adulterous betrothed from this penalty by divorcing her on the quiet.

A further reason, extremely significant, is provided by the expression 'Do not be afraid'. This expression must be taken at its face value, not as 'do not hesitate, do not shrink from'; it is used not of the uneasy conscience, but strictly of fear. Moreover in the new testament the word is used predominantly of a fear or awe at the divine. In Matthew the word means fear of physical violence in chapters 10 and 21, but otherwise (apart from 2:22 and 14:5) it is used nine times of awe at a manifestation of the divine. Especially the negative command 'Do not fear' is used throughout the old and new testaments by a divine messenger to reassure the human interlocutor and to overcome the awe which he feels in the presence of the divine. If, then, the usage here is consistent with the general practice, it must be that Joseph's hesitation to proceed with the marriage is the result of awe at the presence of the divine: he knows that Mary's conception is due to the Spirit of God, and is afraid to put himself forward to be her husband — as well he might be. His decision is the product, not of blind suspicion, but of a reverent sensitivity; this gives perfectly adequate motivation why he should wish quietly to set her free from the betrothal, 'not wanting to draw attention to her'.

What, then, gave rise to the interpretation which revolves round Joseph's suspicion of misconduct by Mary, and does the reason hold any water? It cannot be denied that the last phrase of the words of the angel in verse 21, taken in its most obvious sense, bears this interpretation well: 'Joseph, son of David, do not be afraid to take Mary to yourself as wife, for what has been conceived in her is from the Holy Spirit; but she will bear a son . . . ' This is not good Greek; the 'but' clearly gives an odd sequence of thought, and the 'for' is awkwardly and incorrectly placed in Greek (J.D. Denniston, *The Greek Particles,* 1934, pp 95-8). There is every indication that the author is either translating from or mentally composing in Hebrew or Aramaic. If this is the case it would be rash to build too much on the way the Greek particles are used; the correct use of these notoriously demands a far greater command of the language than any of the evangelists, with the partial exception of Luke, possessed. Besides this, if the phrase is translated back into Aramaic or Hebrew, the resultant phrase could equally well be translated: 'Do not be afraid, on the grounds that what has been conceived in her is from the Holy Spirit, to take Mary to yourself as wife; she will bear a son . . ' The advantage of this translation is that it makes a coherent theological whole of the passage: Joseph is not to be deterred by awe at the divine intervention from going on with his plan of taking Mary to wife; on the contrary, he is not only to do this, he is even to accept the child as his own by naming him.

The virgin birth

Finally, it is impossible in the 1970s to discuss this narrative without at least raising the question of the reality of the virgin birth: can the believer escape from the evangelist's apparent testimony to an occurrence

which is so unpalatable to a scientific age? It has been
said that for a virgin to give birth is impossible or that a
God who breaks the laws of the nature he himself
created is an absurdity. To these claims it is not
proposed to take up any absolute position, but only to
ask whether it seems possible to reconcile them with the
testimony of the evangelist.

On a superficial level attempts have been made to do
away with the testimony of the evangelist: he is simply
taking too literally the biblical quotation which he gives,
'A virgin shall conceive and bear a son'; moreover the
Greek version of Isaiah which he uses is simply a
mis-translation or interpretation, for the original
Hebrew text has merely 'The girl is with child and will
bear a son', without any hint of virgin birth. But this
attempt will not do. The claim that the Greek here
interprets rather than translates the Hebrew is true, but
this cannot be the origin of Matthew's teaching. Firstly,
he is quite capable of using another Greek version if the
Septuagint (the translation he uses here and normally)
does not fit his purpose as well as another version; he
could have done so here unless he already wanted to
bear witness to the virgin birth. Secondly, he uses
scriptural quotations as *Reflexionszitate*, reflection on
the event shows that the scripture is fulfilled; but the
quotation comes after the incident, it does not rule it.
The doctrine of the virgin birth cannot, then, be derived
from the Septuagint Greek of Isaiah.

Another attempt to brush aside the obvious sense of
the gospel is more profound and more biblical. As has
already been remarked, the narrative stands in a series of
biblical stories about wonderful, but not necessarily
strictly miraculous, births. It was almost commonplace

in the bible that a great man who was to do great work for God's people must be born through some special divine intervention, breaking through a barrier of nature such as age or barrenness: the cases of Isaac, Jacob, Samson, John the Baptist spring to mind, It could plausibly be maintained that age and barrenness are tricky factors to assess and no real miracle is involved in any of these — a wonder perhaps, but nothing down-right contrary to the laws of nature. The lesson of all these stories is that the Spirit of God was active in the conception and birth of these children who were later to be moved so specially by the Spirit; but in none of these cases does the activity of the Spirit exclude the activity of man, it rather enhances it and works through it. So the annunciation stories tell us only that the child is, from his conception, to be under the special hand and guidance of God; they do not, at least in the old testament, exclude the normal processes of conception and birth. It may be admitted that this explanation might stand if we had only Luke's story of the annunciation to Mary. A reasonable interpretation of the enigmatic 'since I know not man' could be given, and the rest accounted for as an equivalent of Gen 18, Judges 13 and 1 Sam 1, whose theology of God's action in the world (he is said now to act through his Spirit) is naturally more developed than the theology of those earlier books. But for Matthew this interpretation will not pass: he is explicit that no human intercourse took place, and this makes his task of showing how Jesus was Son of David much harder. One might say that, were it not for the virgin birth, there need have been no story of the annunciation to Joseph.

The naturalistic objector then retreats one step more:

granted that Matthew believed in the physical fact of
the virgin birth, and was not using it merely as a poetic
or symbolic way of expressing that the birth of this
child transcends all normal human bounds, can we say
that he was mistaken here, and must have been
understanding materially what was at an earlier stage
intended in this symbolic sense? One would have to
distinguish here between the fundamental message, the
transcendant origin of Jesus, and the way in which it is
expressed, through the story of the virgin birth. In the
same way one has to distinguish between Paul's message
to await the day of the Lord, and the way in which it is
couched, at any rate by the early Paul, in terms of
imminent cosmic catastrophe. There are certainly places
in the bible where it is necessary thus to distinguish
between the author's fundamental message which all
believers must accept, and the way in which it is
expressed, about which reservations may be made. But
the practice and study of such delicate topics is still in
its very infancy; it would be a brave, and irresponsible,
man who would apply them to the virgin birth of Jesus.

8

Jesus the wonderworker

Of the areas affected by the changed attitude in biblical studies perhaps none has received more of a new look than the area of the miracles of Jesus. In catholic circles a new openness has been made possible by the Instruction of the Biblical Commission in 1964 and its stress on the understanding of literary forms as the only true approach to an ancient text, its insistence that the message of the gospels as expressed in terms which were intended to make its import clear primarily to their own contemporaries, with the consequence that what seems to us to be their meaning at face-value may not always be their true sense. With this change has gone a lessening of emphasis on the apologetic value of the miracles in favour of an increase of attention to their theological meaning; they are regarded no longer as external guarantees of revelation but as a genuine part of it.

The attack by the Bultmann school cannot go and has not gone wholly unnoticed. Of this two-pronged attack the philosophical prong, that miracles simply could not happen, may be disregarded, since it is the christian contention that God simply does intervene in his creation. *Quod gratis affirmatur gratis negatur.* But the literary prong deserves more attention. It is founded on the observation that the miracle-stories of the gospel were formed in a milieu where such stories were the stock-in-trade of any biographer, a normal means by which to show the importance of his subject; even Suetonius' *Lives of the Twelve Caesars* are spattered with them. And as regards cures, a fourth century BC inscription is extant claiming more than sixty cures at the shrine of Aesculapius at Epidaurus in Greece. It is possible to explain away many of these cures as worked through normal medicine or shock or faith-healing under the agency of the temple personnel. But there is something unsatisfactory in this treatment; one feels that different yardsticks are being applied to christian and to pagan claims, or that christian claims are saved from this treatment only because the miracle-stories of the gospel are of a different literary character. Natural-istic explanations have, of course, been given of the miracles, for example when Jesus was thought to be walking on the water he was in fact in the shallow water at the edge of the lake, because when they wanted to take him on board they 'immediately' reached the shore (Jn 6:21). It is impossible to believe that the evangelist meant to leave room for this naturalistic way of understanding, and ridiculous to put on his words an interpretation which, though perhaps not impossible in strict logic, is manifestly contrary to the writer's intentions. One may possibly treat like this a police-court record which claims to be a full and purely factual account; in such cases it may be possible to take individual phrases and use them to contradict the sense intended by the author for the whole, without his being able to expostulate legitimately that this is against his intentions. The situation is obviously different when the story is a schematic popular account. But exactly the same defence can be made of the Epidaurus accounts. In such cases an approach can be made only through the interpretation given to the facts by the author of the account, and so it is of definite importance that the authors of the gospel were living in an atmosphere of credulity, where it was willingly and easily accepted that miracles occurred. A few years before the gospels were written the elder Pliny was told, and believed, the pious Jewish tale that there was in Judaea a brook which observed the sabbath by refusing to flow on that day (Pliny, *Historia Naturalia,* xxxi,18). A fair number of miracles are claimed by the later rabbinic sources, and Josephus tells us that even at the time of Christ false messianic pretenders won adherents by the promise of miracles. Men were certainly more disposed than today to accept happenings as being miraculous.

On the other hand, in part of the tradition about Jesus he is seen to be reticent or even unfavourable in his attitude to miracles. He can rebuke those who seek signs and wonders (Jn 4:48; 6:26), reject those who claim to have done miracles in his name (Mt 7:22). In Mark's gospel almost the only saying of Jesus about miracles is that false Christs will perform them (13:22). The same, interestingly, is true of Mohammed, who does not, according to the Koran, work miracles: 'The unbelievers say, "Why has a sign not been sent down upon him from his Lord?" You are only a warner, and a guide to every people' (*Sura* xiii,8, cf 27). This has not prevented his followers from attributing miracles to him. Similarly in the rabbinic tradition miracles are not regarded with the awe which one might expect; perhaps this is the result of their frequency. In one story the proof-value of miracles appears to be nil: Rabbi Eliezer ben Hyrcanus tries to prove his interpretation of a disputed point by three successive nature-miracles,

which would seem startling enough to us, but leave his
interlocutors unmoved. In another story Rabbi Johanan
ben Zakkai despises a mere miracle-worker: 'He is like a
servant before the king and I am like a nobleman'
(quoted by W. D. Davies, *Setting of the Sermon on the
Mount*, 1966, p 284-5 and 451 respectively). In view of
this it is less surprising that both the Nazarenes and
Herod (Mk 6:2, 14) acknowledge that Jesus does works
of power, but somehow are not thereby induced to
believe in him. The same attitude is reported of the
leaders of the Jews in Jn 11:47.

Works and signs

There are, then, some difficulties about the uniqueness
of Jesus' miracles. We cannot but feel some uneasiness,
some suspicion that we are working from a doctrinaire
position of faith, if we gaily dismiss reports of eg the
claimed miracles at Epidaurus, as does L. Monden (*Signs
and Wonders*, 1966, p 262: 'None of our readers will
find in these cases anything but some purely natural
phenomena'), while accepting the gospel accounts un-
critically at their face value. Furthermore, contemporaries of Christ, and indeed Jesus himself, do not
seem to have regarded the mere fact that an event was
outside the ordinary course of things as overwhelmingly
astounding or as a guarantee of acceptance for one who
performed it. And it follows that if miracle as such
becomes devalued by a flooding of the market, people
are much more unwilling to accept an event as miraculous, and miracles multiply even more. As regards the
gospels, the lack of concentration on the miraculous

character as such is confirmed by the observation that
the gospels have no word for 'miracle'. The most likely
candidate is *dynamis* (literally 'power'), used thirty-
seven times by the synoptics (never by John) to refer to
what we would call miracles twelve times, to include
miracles six times, but otherwise of actions which we
would not regard as miraculous. The Johannine equivalent is (in Jesus' mouth) *ergon,* a neutral word meaning
'work' and used up to fifteen times of miracles but
certainly twelve times in a more general sense, or
semeion (literally 'sign'); this is used seventeen times by
John, in the majority of cases including miracles in its
reference; but it cannot be said to mean 'a miracle' or
even 'a miraculous sign'. The only obvious word for
'miracle' is *teras,* which is indeed used in this sense nine
times in the Acts; but it occurs for the works of Jesus
only in Jn 4:48, and is elsewhere used only of cosmic
portents in the heavens (Mk 13:22; Mt 24:24). It
becomes, therefore, questionable whether we should use
the unevangelical expression 'miracle' of the actions of
Jesus in the gospel at all.

But if the purpose of Jesus' works is not to be found
in the mere fact that they attract attention by their
miraculousness — rather like a conjuring trick, where it
does not matter whether a rabbit or a pigeon is
produced out of a hat, but what does matter is that
something inexplicable to the audience is performed —
their significance must be sought not in the fact of the
'work' but in its nature. Here, as so often, John the
theologian makes clear what remains only implicit in the
synoptics by calling them 'signs'. By so doing he places
them in continuity with the prophetic acted signs of the
old testament, by which prophets, especially Jeremiah

and Ezekiel but also many of the non-literary prophets of the Book of Kings, communicated their message of revelation. These signs are not guarantors but are vehicles of revelation. So also Jesus' signs are not just random actions showing extraordinary superiority to nature, but are directed to revealing specific aspects of his person. It is this that the evangelists wish to bring out in their narratives; but since, at any rate in the synoptics, this is done largely by reference to the old testament, showing how Jesus repeats in a higher way in his own person a great figure of the old law, and since this method of implicit allusion and contrast seems from an early date to have been misunderstood or forgotten, the original sense of the 'signs' was lost, and all emphasis came to be placed on their wonderful or miraculous character.

An interpretation of the 'works of Christ' which may well be Jesus' own is given in one of the very few passages of Q (the collection of sayings of the Lord used as a source by both Matthew and Luke) where the sayings are combined with narrative: Mt 11:2-6, Lk 7:18-23. Jesus sends a message to the imprisoned John the Baptist, showing in what way he is the messiah, by describing his works of healing in terms deliberately reminiscent of the Book of Isaiah's description of the messianic age. The sense, then, of these works of healing is as signs that the messianic age has dawned. The same sense is given to the expulsion of demons in Mk 3:23-7, cf Mt 12:25-9, Lk 11:17-22. But here the declaration is framed in different terms, which must be viewed against the background of the popular acceptance of a ubiquitous world of spirits current at the time, attested, eg, by the Qumran documents. According to these, the two spirits of truth and of perversity exist in the world, but at the end of time the spirit of perversity will be banished and the spirit of truth will triumph (*Rule of the Community* III, 20-1, cf *Book of Mysteries* I, 5). Thus Jesus' expulsion of demons shows that the last times have arrived, in which the evil spirits will be cast out. For the men of Jesus' time a connexion was taken for granted between sickness and evil spirits and moral evil, or rather both moral and physical evil were expressed in terms of evil spirits. This frame of reference Jesus used, and presumably shared, showing that he ushered in the messianic kingdom which was to overcome evil and 'wipe away every tear' (Is 24:8; Rev 21:4), for the messianic kingdom was to introduce a return to the paradisiac state, when no evil, either physical or moral, survived, and of this Jesus' 'works' are signs.

The effect of personality

It is tempting to give a psychological explanation of the works of healing which would run on these lines. Some people of extraordinary or forceful personality have a power over others through some sort of non-physical power. The possible limits of psychic influence are still ill-defined. The personality of Jesus was undoubtedly striking beyond all comparison, so that he might be expected to achieve healing effects beyond the limit of treatments otherwise known. It is remarkable that many of his cures are effected on those suffering from nervous disorders, eg the Gadarene demoniac and the epileptic boy, or those suffering from unspecified skin diseases (*lepra* does not mean leprosy in the modern sense, but can be used much more widely, eg 'a swelling or scab or shiny spot', Lev 13:1) or merely confined to bed (such is the meaning of *paralyticos*). Any of these might be in the classes of maladies which could be cured by the influence of an overwhelming personality such as Jesus must have possessed. Nor are these cures to be dismissed as *merely* faith-healing; they could be classified as properly theandric actions: the godhead in Jesus is acting in a human key, through the manhood in a way proper to man, using his human personality to produce effects analogous to, but greatly enhanced above, effects produced by contact with other forceful but merely human personalities. They really do show what the translation of the divinity into human terms could mean. Attractive as this explanation is, it is at best partial, for it cannot include all the works of Jesus, namely those for which there is no possibility of psychological effect from his personality on a subject, such as the raising of the dead, the multiplication of loaves, the calming of the storm.

The works of God

But it is certainly significant that there are the cases where the full meaning and message of the event is most closely dependent on their biblical background. One of the important purposes of the synoptic evangelists is to show that Jesus is a prophet, or rather the prophet foretold by Moses (Deut 18:15, 18), since he repeats their actions. The raising of the dead was certainly referred back to the stories of Elijah and Elisha in 1 Kg

17:17-24 and 2 Kg 4:28-37; as they raised to life the
only son of a widow, so did Jesus, after which he is
hailed specifically as a prophet (Lk 7:16). There is,
however, surely also a further overtone which would be
obvious to a reader conversant with the bible: only God
gives life (Gen 30:2; Deut 32:39; 1 Sam 2:6; Ps 30:3; 2
Kg 5:7), and so by giving life Jesus implicitly claims to
accomplish the works of God, as in Jn 5:21. The same
claim is implicit in the two miracles on the lake, the
walking on the water and the calming of the storm, for
the sea had always been thought of by the Hebrews as
an evil, destructive power, recalling the waters of chaos,
and restrained only through the power of God. Liberation by God from evil powers is frequently described as
liberation from deep waters, and conversely calming of a
storm at sea is regarded as a major proof of God's love
(Job 7:12; 22:10-11; Ps 74:13; 18:4; 107:23-30).
Walking on the waves is specifically a divine prerogative
(Job 9:8; Sir 24:5; Ps 77:19).

These actions are not, then, random conjuring tricks,
but are highly symbolic, revealing a definite and
well-defined aspect of Christ's person. The question is
bound to arise, to what extent have the evangelists or
the community before them formed the narratives,
interpreted the original events which are their basis, in
order to bring out these aspects of Christ with all
possible clarity? Work which has been done on the
narrative of the multiplication of loaves will provide
valuable evidence here (cf A. Heising, *Die Botschaft der
Brotvermehrung*, 1966). This narrative, which seems so
simple and spontaneous (Mk 6:30-44), is in fact
carefully formed to bring out its messianic meaning.
Prominent is the parallelism with a similar wonderful

feeding by Elisha in 2 Kg 4:42-4; this is especially true of the dialogue between Jesus and the disciples, which exactly corresponds to the progress of the dialogue between Elisha and his disciple; the purpose of this is again to show Jesus as a prophet repeating and overshadowing the works of Elisha. But other details too are meaningful: the 'green grass' (6:39 — odd in a 'desert place', verse 31) probably recalls the meadows of green grass where the messianic shepherd of Ps 23 is to feed his flock. Even the numbers are probably symbolic, for the men are grouped into hundreds and fifties, groupings which were used for the messianic community in the writings of Qumran (1 QS II, 22; 1 QM IV, 3, etc), and which may again be intended to indicate the messianic character of this meal. The ease with which the evangelists exaggerate the size of crowds may be illustrated by Matthew's treatment of the 'Palm Sunday' entry into Jerusalem, where he changes Mark's 'many people' into a 'huge crowd' (Mt 21:8) and 'those who went in front and who followed' into 'the crowds who went in front and who followed'. When these and the clearly posterior eucharistic details are eliminated there remains a substratum of an event which it is by no means easy to isolate. It is possible to assume that there is some incident at the basis of the story, though its exact nature is difficult or impossible to determine now; but it can also be maintained that the story has been generated by the combination of two factors, the knowledge that Jesus as messiah was a prophet, the culmination of the line of previous prophets, and the memory that he worked wonders. Some generalised and summary accounts of cures are surely the product of this memory; they are founded on the general memory of his work rather than on that of any particular incident (eg Mt 8:16-17; Lk 7:21). It is perhaps not too much to suppose that, when this technique was applied to Jesus' role as the last and greatest of the line of prophets, quite a trivial incident may have been seen in this light as a sign, and described in a way which both brings out this aspect of Jesus and uses the knowledge that he did do such remarkable signs.

The attempt has been made in this chapter to view the 'powerful works' of Jesus less as isolated incidents, valuable in themselves, than as indications to the meaning of his whole person, to be taken all together, signs of his function of eschatological fulfilment and at the same time pointers to a still higher role. In the context of the ease with which actions were hailed as miraculous, and of the literary conventions through which the nature of Jesus was expressed by the evangelists, it is legitimate to ask of any single 'work of power' whether the deed on which the story is founded was in fact miraculous. Jesus' own few recorded sayings about 'signs and wonders' might further give rise to some hesitations about the miracle tradition as a whole. Was the resurrection the only miracle? But though doubt about the miraculousness of any single 'work' is perhaps legitimate, it does seem foolhardy to attempt radically to reinterpret a whole structure so deep-rooted and widespread in the gospel tradition.

9

Jesus the teacher

A quest which has pervaded these pages is for the
theological message which the biblical authors intended
to convey by their narration of events, and a fair
number of different literary patterns and conventions
have been discussed. In the last analysis, however, the
meaning of events told in the gospels must come from
Jesus himself. Of course the understanding of his
message by the twelve under the guidance of the Spirit
developed. Theology is a developing process, and of no
stage of the church's history can this be more true than
of the first crucial moment. Hence the apostles, and
later the community and the evangelists, came to
express Jesus's teaching in words and by means which
were not necessarily his own. It may even be possible to
ask here whether Jesus himself always fully understood
the deepest implications of his own actions, actions
whose meaning the earliest community came to understand fully only in the light of prolonged meditation on
the scriptures. As man it belonged to the fullness of the
perfection of Jesus that he should learn, and himself
develop and grow more profound until he was finally
perfected in obedience by suffering (Heb 5:8). As other
men grow in self-awareness, and realise the full significance of their actions, and even sometimes of their
words, only with the passage of time, can we not
envisage Jesus too growing in this way? Nevertheless,

though penetration of the message increased as time went on, the impetus must have begun with Jesus.

It is when we attempt to progress from this theological statement to its practical application in the matter of what Jesus himself actually taught that controversy begins. The Council *Decree on Revelation* 19 (clearly based on the 1964 Instruction of the Biblical Commission on the historicity of the gospels) happily grants that the apostles 'selected', 'reduced to a synthesis', 'explained in view of the situation of the communities', insisting only that they tell 'the honest truth about Jesus . . . what he really did and taught'. There is stress upon fidelity, but not upon verbal exactitude. On the contrary, it seems fairly clear that words which had a certain sense to a Jewish country audience under certain circumstances might well be misleading, or carry a different sense to the gentile hellenistic city-dwellers who formed the majority in the early christian community; similarly reduction to a synthesis and explanation in view of a different situation do suggest at any rate the possibility of verbal change.

Once this possibility has been admitted then a whole new task is laid before the biblical scholar (the biblical scholar, not necessarily the exegete, since for exegesis proper it can often be irrelevant whether the wording is that of Jesus or of his faithful interpreters), and two opposing angles of approach are open. Either it is assumed that the words are those of Jesus unless the contrary is proved, or nothing is taken to be from Jesus's own lips unless it is definitely established to be so. The former, positive, attitude has generally been characteristic of the catholic tradition, the latter, agnostic, that of the liberal scholar.

Did the early church retain Jesus's own words?

A very firm recent exponent of this latter position is Norman Perrin in his book *Rediscovering the Teaching of Jesus* (London, 1967). He sets out to justify his position from two directions, *a priori* and *a posteriori*. *A priori*, 'The early Church made no attempt to distinguish between the words the earthly Jesus had spoken and those spoken by the risen Lord through a prophet in the community. . . . The early Church absolutely and completely identified the risen Lord of her experience with the earthly Jesus of Nazareth' (p 16). The foundation for this assertion seems to be the narrative in the Acts of the Apostles of Paul's conversion, and Paul's own reference, presumably to this incident, in 1 Cor 15:8. There the risen Lord is treated quite simply as 'the Lord' without distinction from the earthly Jesus. A more convincing passage, often used for this purpose, is Ac 13:2. 'While they were offering worship to the Lord and keeping a fast the Holy Spirit said, "I want Barnabas and Saul set apart for the work to which I have called them" '. Here is a saying, pronounced no doubt by one of the prophets mentioned in the previous verse, which is ascribed at any rate to the Holy Spirit in connexion with worship to the Lord; it is only a step from here to saying that this is a word of the Lord himself — a step which is, incidentally, not taken. On the contrary, Paul seems to distinguish firmly between what the Lord said and what he himself says, for all his gifts of the Spirit: 'I myself have no directions from the Lord but give my own opinion' (1 Cor 7:25). A third *a priori* argument used by Perrin is the equivalence of the expressions 'eyewitness' in Lk

1:2 and 'witness' to the Lord, which Paul uses of himself in Ac 22:15 and 26:16, thereby suggesting that the claimed eyewitness testimony to Jesus's words and deeds in the gospel is no more than Paul's witness to Jesus; this of course is entirely without foundation, for in Greek the two words have totally different roots and usages.

The *a priori* arguments of Perrin are, then, weak; but are the *a priori* arguments for the 'catholic' assumption any stronger? The two most usual arguments are not very powerful. The early christians, it is said, were concerned to preserve the memory of Jesus faithfully; but this begs the question of the meaning of 'faithfully', which does not necessarily mean 'with slavish literalness'. Secondly, it is claimed that the early community did not have sufficient inventiveness to compose sayings of Jesus in which they assert what they considered that he would have said in certain circumstances; this claim is so vague and depends on so many imponderables that it deserves little consideration. Scandinavian scholars (notably B. Gerhardsson in his *Memory and Manuscript*, 1961) have, however, strengthened the case by an examination of teaching techniques in judaism. In spite of the heavy criticism levelled against his treatment of individual new testament passages, his study of the widespread use of memorisation and verbally exact transmission of the sayings of teachers has shown that it was at least possible that Jesus's sayings should be handed down with minute accuracy; but of course these background studies deal with communities which did not feel themselves to be under the régime of the Spirit and where prophecy was notably lacking. In communities like the early christian ones where the Spirit

was constantly felt to be active, the Jewish method of
passing on tradition by memorisation need not have
been the only form of transmission of the christian
message.

Which were the sayings of Jesus?

On the basis of the *a priori* arguments, then, no firm
decision about the verbal exactitude of the reporting of
Jesus's sayings is justified. Decision can be made only *a
posteriori*, by examining the sayings themselves. Here
Perrin asserts 'Contemporary scholarship has explained
pericope after pericope on the basis of the needs and
concerns of the early Church' (p 16), 'every single
parable in the tradition has to be approached with the
basic assumption that, as it now stands, it represents the
teaching of the early Church' (p 21). He cites at length
discussions of three particular passages where this
appears to be the case. The basic forms of argumenta-
tion behind all such attempts can perhaps be reduced to
two: a passage reflects a preoccupation which could
arise only in the early church, not in the life of Jesus (eg
official persecution by the Jews and expulsion from
their synagogues; this did not occur in the earliest days
of the church, and it would be strange if the disciples
had continued to frequent the synagogues and to
attempt to conform to Jewish customs if they knew
beforehand that they were to be expelled), or it reflects
a dogmatic awareness which was reached only after the
resurrection (eg Peter's confession 'Truly you are the
Son of God' in Mt 14:33, even long before Caesarea
Philippi). The other argument works from a comparison

of the different versions of a saying in different gospels, especially the synoptics, where it is often quite clear that Matthew and Luke make slight alterations, the better to express their own theological preoccupations. Further, it may be argued, if Matthew and Luke edit the wording of sayings of Jesus, Mark also probably does so, thus destroying all access to the original saying; the editing is, of course, harder to detect in Mark's case, since we do not possess the version on which he is working. But in the case of sayings where this latter argument is employed we are not justified in claiming that the saying has *necessarily* been composed by the evangelist, for it is possible that there already existed a saying which he received from the tradition and worked on.

The advances of modern scholarship make it impossible not to grant that there are at least some instances in which sayings which purport to be sayings of the Lord are in fact not *verbatim* from Jesus's lips. The question therefore arises, if we are to consider Jesus as a teacher, which are and which are not his own sayings? Perrin works out three criteria which are intended to guarantee that a saying which passes any of them must be an authentic saying of Jesus. The first and most important of these is the criterion of dissimilarity (p 39): a saying is authentic if it is 'dissimilar to characteristic emphases both of ancient Judaism and of the early Church', for then it is not likely to stem from either of them. By this criterion a number of authentic sayings would surely be excluded, unless we are to suppose that Jesus never echoed the emphases of judaism, nor — which would be still more surprising — the early church those of Jesus! The criterion is too stringent. The second criterion, that of coherence with material accepted on the first criterion, requires no comment. The third, the criterion of multiple attestation, is put forward only with hesitation: if material is attested in all, or most, of the sources of the gospel it is assumed to stem from Jesus. But the trouble here is that strictly this justifies no further conclusion than that the material stems from a source sufficiently ancient to be accepted by a large part of the tradition, but not that this source is Jesus himself. It seems, then, that a perfectly satisfactory scientific instrument has yet to be forged for discerning with certainty the sayings of Jesus.

Editorial tendencies

Nevertheless, even if individual sayings of Jesus cannot always be picked out, it is possible to isolate certain emphases in the gospel message which do seem to be the result of later meditation on the person of Jesus. The principal tendency at work is, of course, clarification, a concern to express more clearly some aspects which Jesus himself left inexplicit, and especially to point more clearly to the person of Jesus and to show in more detail his knowledge and control of events. The first of these shows itself very clearly in the parables; if anything is clear from J. Jeremias's great book on the parables (*The Parables of Jesus,* London, 1963) it is the tendency which he names 'christological allegorisation' (p 66 ff). In the parables where Jesus taught about the kingdom, the evangelists have by subtle touches thrown the emphasis on to its proclaimer, Jesus. Thus the original sense of the parable of the talents concerned the use and abuse of God's gifts, no doubt applied to those of the Jews, the leaders, who considered themselves superior to the common run of men, and whom Jesus reproaches for failure to use their advantages in preparing for the coming of the kingdom. But in the gospels, interested as they are in the return of Christ to judge the world, the moment of the parable is transferred to the end of the world and the stress on to the person of Jesus. Similarly the parable of the wicked husbandmen was originally intended to suggest to the hearers that those in charge of the vineyard of the Lord had failed in their office; but the evangelists add the allegorising details which make the climax of the story the killing of Jesus and the resultant punishment for rejecting the cornerstone. In these and similar passages it cannot be said that the evangelists distort the message of Jesus or get it wrong; they are faithful to the message, but if we are to discover the content and method of Jesus's own teaching we must return to a more primitive state of the tradition.

The same process of explicitation occurs with regard to the shorter sayings of Jesus. Two examples of this can be traced if we take Mark's gospel as the original version and the other two synoptics as expanded versions. In the controversy about Satan and the spirit of Jesus in Mk 3:23-30, Jesus throws down a series of images, the divided kingdom, the divided household and the strong man on guard. He does not explain in detail, but leaves his hearers to reflect on them (we need not suppose that all were pronounced on the same occasion). There is no reference to himself or to the king or bringer of the kingdom, only to the kingdom itself; the hearers are provoked to reflect not directly on Jesus's

person but upon the era of the breaking out of God's
kingship. It is only with Matthew and Luke that the
reference to Jesus himself comes. Similarly in the
controversy over a sign; Mk 8:11-13 says that no sign
shall be given, but the versions in Matthew and Luke
make an exception: the sign of the prophet Jonah will
be given — an obvious reference to the death and
resurrection of Jesus. For the detailing of events, the
most obvious case is the three great prophecies of the
passion given in the second half of the gospel. As these
now stand they are far more detailed and explicit than
we can suppose them to have been on Jesus's lips, but
on the other hand it is impossible to suppose that Jesus
had no foreknowledge that he would be arrested and
killed, or that he did not share this knowledge with his
disciples. A middle position is necessary: basically the
message is that of Jesus, but it is made more explicit in
view of the increased understanding of the disciples
after the resurrection.

If we are to have positive criteria for sayings which
stem from Jesus, there are rough guides, less scientific
than those of Norman Perrin, but still useful. There
seem to me to be at least two likely hallmarks of Jesus's
sayings. One is that they breathe the air of the
Palestinian countryside. There is a large number of such
sayings in the synoptic tradition, many of the parables
and similes, stories such as those about plucking ears of
corn or pulling oxen out of pits, which show one who
knew and loved the countryside and agriculture as only
a villager can. These could never have originated in the
urban communities where early christianity flourished,
in the circles indicated by the language and special
interests of the evangelists. Another hallmark could be

the rhythmic and balancing form of a saying. We know that Jesus was an inspired (also in the non-theological sense) oral teacher, and much of the power of such a teacher lies in his ability to frame his message in lapidary and pithy sayings. There is this quality in many of the gospel sayings, together with a balance which is characteristic of Hebrew thought: this form can be clearly seen in the way the sayings are set out by Robert Petitpierre in his *Poems of Jesus* (Faith Press, 1965). But this latter characteristic is no more than an indication pointing towards authenticity; it is no sure sign, for there were other inspired oral teachers who couched their message in terms natural to Hebrew thought. A third characteristic of Jesus's teaching which has long been recognised is his tendency to break off, leaving a question echoing in the mind of the listener. He does not provide all the answers, but leaves it, with the tact of the confident teacher, to the well-intentioned listener to draw out the lesson from the parable or question which he puts. This feature is not always useful for distinguishing authentic sayings, for the early church, concerned above all to clarify, has often overlaid this open-endedness with a definite answer; but it does throw valuable light on his teaching method.

The kingship of God

It is impossible in a treatment of this length, and especially after such a lengthy discussion of preliminaries, even to begin to outline the content of Jesus's teaching. No more can be done than to say that a

very central point was the kingdom. This is not a
territorial concept but a dynamic reality, for the form
of the Hebrew noun underlying it, *malkuth,* shows that
it is a verbal noun, 'the being king' of God. This
spearhead of Jewish hope meant the realisation of God's
being king on earth. In the old testament and afterwards
it is an idea which gradually develops, gathering more
and more significance and richness: basically it is the act
of God on the 'day of the Lord' at the end of time,
when he makes the great visitation on the world,
concluding all things, punishing and rewarding in his
loving tenderness. Gradually it is seen that this involves
such things as the transformation of the world, the
return of the paradisal state, the resurrection of the
dead and the end of significant history. The ways and
the imaginative forms in which this event of all events is
expressed are legion. The crux of Jesus's teaching is that
this day has arrived. But he has to prune drastically the
implications — widely varied and highly complex —
which this carried in the minds of his contemporaries,
and to substitute new ones. This is the purpose of so
many of his parables: it bursts the bonds of old judaism
(new wine in new wineskins, no new patch on old
clothes), it is not to be reached by the path of the
pharisees (the wicked husbandmen), it can come bringing fear and trembling (the great supper) for it comes
unexpectedly like a thief in the night. It is not the
triumphalist rule that many of the Jews expected, and a
number of the parables are directed to explaining the
paradox that this outbreak of the rule of God on earth
makes no great or obvious stir, but begins in littleness,
growing only gradually to its full extent (the mustard
seed, the leaven). A further paradox was that the

associates of Jesus were not those whom Jewish piety expected to be the partners in God's rule, but were lost sheep and prodigal sons. It was not an event which just happened to a person willy-nilly like the apparition of a *deus ex machina*, but needed the active co-operation of men (the two sons, one of whom is obedient, the other of whom merely protests obedience; the sulky children in the market-place who refuse to dance no matter what tune is played).

This stress on the present breaking-in of God's rule on earth is balanced in Jesus's preaching by statements about the future of God's rule on earth. There are enough of these that bear the hallmarks of Jesus's own words to show that he did teach about it, although it was undeniably an interest of the synoptic evangelists, particularly Matthew, to enlarge and emphasise the teaching about the second coming, the last judgement and the consummation of all things. Nevertheless if we take the key to the understanding of Jesus's good news to be the realisation of God's rule in the moment of his coming and preaching, we have a central stance from which the rest of his teaching may be understood in its true perspective.

10

The crucifixion of Jesus

I

The narrative of Jesus's passion and death is of course the most important of all the gospel stories, the one which has most engaged the devotion and meditation of christians from the earliest days. Because of its crucial importance the community through whose hands it passed, and the evangelists who finally passed it on to us, were concerned to interpret it to us as clearly as possible.

One of the principal ways in which the meaning of events in the life of Jesus was seen was by reference to the old testament, and especially is this the case with the passion, for this contained the great scandal, the humiliation and death of the messiah, an essentially glorious and resplendent figure. Therefore it was important to show that this humiliation was directly intended by God, and announced by him in the scriptures. Frequently in the new testament, and seemingly already in the sayings of Jesus himself, the passages appealed to for this purpose are those about the servant of the Lord in Isaiah, who reaches triumphal vindication after suffering and humiliation innocently borne for the atonement of the sins of others. In the passion narrative, however, it is more the psalms which are pressed into

service. Some, for instance Ps 21, have a similar theme
to the suffering servant poems; others are more remote
but are used on the grounds that Christ is the fulfilment
of the whole of the old testament, and therefore the
whole of the old testament, and every individual passage
in it, speaks of Christ, a principle which would be
disputed by modern exegetes, deep-rooted though it be
in the approach of the early church and the typological
school of interpreters; the old testament is as a whole
fulfilled in Christ, but it does not follow that each
individual passage points to him directly.

Psalm 21

Perhaps the most important citation of the psalms is
that of the opening of Ps 21 as Jesus's last words in
Mark and Matthew. The interpretation of this as a cry of
dereliction, as though Jesus were suffering the pains of
the damned in total separation from God, though it was
for so long current in christian piety, is quite at variance
at least with any Pauline theology, according to which
the moment of Christ's death is that at which his union
to the Father in loving obedience is so intense that it
undoes Adam's separation from God in disobedience. In
view of the prominence of the whole of the psalm in the
passion narrative it is much more likely that the
evangelists understood the quotation as the intonation
of the psalm as a whole; by intoning the psalm Jesus
gives his own interpretation of his death, for the
movement of the psalm parallels that of the suffering
servant song: through humiliation to vindication and the
glory of God. To what extent the words are an

interpretation of the 'great cry' with which Jesus
expired is also perhaps questionable. The confusion
about Elijah could hardly have arisen if he cried 'Elohi,
Elohi, lama sabachthani' as in Mark, for to anyone of
sufficient biblical culture to think of Elijah the psalm
verse would have been more obvious. One is tempted to
think that the cry for Elijah and the psalm are two
originally alternative interpretations of what was in fact
the inarticulate cry of a dying man. Luke gives a third
alternative in another quotation from a psalm, 'Into
your hands I commend my spirit'.

Once the suitability of Ps 21 as an aid to the
interpretation of the crucifixion is established it may be
seen reflected in many incidents in the narrative. For
instance, the division of Jesus's clothes among the
soldiers is described by means of a quotation from the
psalm; John even makes a distinction between his outer
garments and his tunic in order that each half of the
verse may be fulfilled separately, 'They divide my
garments among them and cast lots for my clothing'.
The mockery by his enemies similarly is seen as a
fulfilment of this psalm by Mark and Matthew when
they jeer at him 'tossing their heads' (Ps 21:8); Matthew
even puts the words of those who mock the just man
into their mouths, 'He relied on God, let God save him
if he is his friend' (Ps 21:9), though it is hardly likely
that the doctors of the law should so ostentatiously
condemn themselves by using the words of the enemies
of God's servant; to the evangelist, however, it serves to
point the similarity once more.

The details of historical fact are of comparative
unimportance beside the fulfilment of the scripture.
Matthew feels himself to be quite justified in altering

Mark's 'wine mixed with myrrh' which Jesus is offered
on the way to the cross for 'wine mixed with gall' in
order to fulfil Ps 68:22. Mark's version is wholly
probable, for there existed a custom by which some
women offered a narcotic to condemned prisoners on
their way to execution, and for this myrrh would be
suitable, but not Matthew's gall. The discovery of such a
tendency deliberately to conform details of the events
to the psalms must give rise at least to speculation
whether other minor incidents where a psalm is not
explicitly quoted may not show the effect of the
psalms. A case in point is the two thieves. The
differentiation between them occurs only in Luke, and
this element is so characteristic of him that it must
surely originate with him the vocabulary and style show
the sophistication which distinguishes him from the
other evangelists, and the stress on Jesus's forgiveness of
the repentant even in direst agony befits the writer of
the stories of the prodigal son, the woman who was a
sinner and of the pharisee and the tax-collector in the
temple. In all these stories of Luke there is also the
contrast between two figures, one repentant, the other
unrepentant and contemptuous. (A similar theme is
given also in the textually doubtful 'Forgive them,
Father, for they do not know what they are doing',
which is missing in some manuscripts.) This is Luke's
way of underlining that the forgiveness of sinners is the
meaning of the cross; as this gives the clue to Jesus's
ministry, so it reaches its climax in his death. One
wonders, however, whether the presence of the two
thieves on either side of Jesus is not connected with Ps
21 again, for verse 17 has 'the gathering of evil men
surrounds me'; this could be the reason for the stress in

all evangelists that they are on either side of Jesus.

II

It is not only by the human incidents that we may expect to discover the meaning which the evangelists saw in the crucifixion, but also by the phenomena of nature, for it was especially in these that the biblical tradition saw the finger of God. There are four remarkable phenomena mentioned, and of these three receive their explanation as fulfilment of scripture. The fourth, the rending of the temple veil, relates to a more recent tradition attested also by the Jewish historian, Josephus. He tells that four years before the destruction of Jerusalem (other sources have the figure forty, symbolic of an indefinite period) the great doors of the temple flew open, untouched by hand. This must surely correspond to the vision of Ez 10:18-19, in which the prophet sees the glory of the Lord leave the temple shortly before its first destruction by Babylonian forces. The rending of the veil may well be an alternative version of such a symbolism: with the death of Jesus the destruction of the old Israel is sealed and the glory of God leaves the holy of holies.

In the case of the natural phenomena we shall hardly penetrate to a deeper understanding of the crucifixion by attempting to explain the darkness over the earth by an unnaturally intense spring dust-storm or by consulting the records of eclipses and earthquakes. Basically they are ways of showing the cosmic significance of the events to which even nature responds; but, further, they are sanctioned by biblical prophecies. Darkness at

midday had, since the beginning of apocalyptic writing
with Amos, shown poetically the mourning and terror
of the world at the eschatological day of the Lord.
Earthquake also is a recognised sign in Hebrew poetry of
the coming of the Lord at whose footstep earth
trembles. The juxtaposition in Matthew of this element
with the foretaste of the general resurrection (27:51-3)
may well illustrate his theme of the old and new Israel,
for he often stresses the two nations of Israel, the old
Israel now superseded by the new Israel of God;
earthquake is used often in the old testament of the
prelude and accompaniment of God's visitation to
destroy a sinful nation; and the resurrection of many
who are already dead is reminiscent of the prophecy of
the resurrection of Israel in the valley of the dry bones
(Ez 37:1-14), though the wording is much more similar
to the prophecy of individual resurrection in Isaiah
26:19. By these two additions of his to Mark's account,
Matthew is, then, showing that it is the moment of
Christ's death that supersedes the old people of Israel
and begins the new world of the resurrection.

John

The fourth gospel supplies its own interpretation of the
crucifixion by means of two highly pregnant scriptural
texts attached to incidents which would be in themselves quite trivial, did they not reflect old testament
passages. These are the facts that they did not break
Jesus's legs according to the normal practice, and that
blood and water flowed from his side. John places
tremendous emphasis on this phenomenon, but what-

ever its medical explanation it cannot be intended as proof that he was dead. John was not interested in the point at such a trivial level, and his stress on the reliability of the witness to it relates to the symbolic and scriptural meaning; he concludes: 'that you too may believe, for these things happened in order to fulfil the scriptures'. Both of the citations which follow pick up and round off a theme which has already been prominent in the gospel. The former, 'Not a bone is to be broken', probably concludes the series of quiet references in John to the paschal lamb, which began as soon as Jesus appeared, with the Baptist's 'This is the lamb of God'. The latter citation, 'They shall look on him whom they have pierced', is less obvious but even richer in Johannine symbolism. Of Jesus's actual death John had written 'he gave forth the spirit', a typically Johannine double-sense which interprets his death as the moment at which he gave his promised Spirit to mankind: as he goes away he sends the Paraclete who is to be with his disciples always. Now this is reinforced, for water is to John the symbol of the life given by the Spirit; there is an unmistakable link with Jesus's cry in Jn 7:38-9: 'Let the man come and drink who believes in me. As scripture says, "From his breast shall flow fountains of living water".' The promise to give water runs through the gospel, baptism in water and the Spirit to Nicodemus, the promise of living water to the Samaritan woman. Both water and Spirit come in the prophecy of Zechariah, which provides the latter quotation at the crucifixion; so John wishes to show that by the crucifixion Zechariah's promise is fulfilled that in the last times God 'will pour out a spirit of kindness and prayer' and 'a fountain will be opened for sin and impurity' (12:10 and 13:1); it is the moment of the birth of God's renewed and eschatological community. It is this that provides the reason for John's insistence on the reliability of his witness at this moment.

The motive of the soldier's action is difficult to understand in John's account. The reason for not breaking his legs was that they saw he was already dead, so it cannot have been to ensure his death. Besides this, the word used for the wounding does not indicate a deep thrust, but more a slight prick ('to *prick* the lion in his den', or 'a *stinging* reply'); it could be a purely gratuitous and callous prick with a lance. It would be interesting to establish a connexion with the soldier mentioned in the synoptic accounts just after Jesus's death; he also gives a testimony for the faith, though of course much more directly. John's account shows the founding of the church, while that of the synoptics seems to have similar significance: immediately after the rending of the veil of the temple — the revelation of the emptiness of the temple cult of judaism — a leader of the gentiles declares what to the evangelists is his faith, signifying the entry of the gentiles into the community of faith. During his life Jesus's mission was to the Jews, but immediately at his death it spreads to the gentiles. Matthew emphasises the point: not only is it the centurion who testifies but those with him too, and all are filled with a divine awe; this too may be seen in function of Matthew's theological theme of the re-placement of the community of Israel by a new community of disciples which includes the gentiles. Luke, with characteristic generosity in his universalism, spreads it still further: all the crowds of passers-by beat their breasts in repentance.

III

The question must finally be raised about the nature of the evidence. The basic scene which would be normal for such an execution is comparatively easy to visualise. The very early traditional site of the execution is on a slight elevation some fifty yards outside the city gate, beside the road leading out of Jerusalem to the coast. Crucifixions beside a road were a normal practice, for then the criminal had the additional distress of public mockery, and the public also benefitted from the warning in seeing the penalty for crime. Crucifixion was, after all, the standard form of execution for slaves convicted of insurrection, and would be eminently suitable for a provincial charged with — if hardly convicted of — setting himself up as messiah. If anything is clear about the legalities of the trial scenes, it is that the Jews are trying to fasten on to Jesus, and frighten Pilate into accepting, the charge of setting himself up as the sort of messianic claimant already well known in Palestine, who attempted to overthrow the Romans and found a messianic state. That a placard specifying the offence should be attached to the gibbet is not in itself surprising, and is attested for other cases at this time. The Johannine version, according to which Pilate himself takes a hand in the writing of it (and seemingly at Golgotha itself, since there is no sign of coming and going) and thereby seems personally to acknowledge Jesus's real kingship, and indeed proclaim it officially to the world, is perhaps more theological than historical, for John brings out throughout the passion narrative that Jesus's kingship is now finally recognised and eventually proclaimed by his enthronement on the

cross. The stripping and division of the clothes are
entirely plausible, for the Romans crucified naked and
the clothes belonged by custom to the soldiers charged
with the execution; it has been suggested that in Judaea
they would moderate this to allow for the Jews'
susceptibilities in this respect (2 Macc 4:9, 12) so far as
to leave some undergarment, but no ancient text
suggests this.

The real questions begin to be asked after this: how
factual is the account of Jesus's last hours on the cross?
The Roman guard was presumably intended to keep the
execution scene free of the victim's well-wishers, and
even this is seen as the fulfilment of scripture, namely Ps
38, 'My friends and my companions shrink from my
wounds, even the dearest of them keep their distance':
the verse is quoted by Luke but implied also by Mark
and Matthew. We have seen that the desire to show the
fulfilment of scripture was responsible for certain details
of the account of Jesus's last hours; the question arises
how far this may be the case. If the incidents correspond to the scriptures one of two alternatives must
be chosen: either the story was created by the conviction that the scriptures must be fulfilled and that certain
psalm verses *must* have been fulfilled on the cross, or
the correspondence of historical incidents to the scriptures has led to their preservation in the account. A
fundamental presupposition of modern biblical scholarship, which has also been basic to this series of articles,
is that the former alternative cannot be ruled out *a
priori*. One of the evangelists' methods of teaching was
to embroider the tradition they received with minor
details, to bring out aspects of Jesus and of his teaching
which, under the holy Spirit, they or their community

believed to be of importance. It would clearly be rash to assume the former alternative for each case; one cannot rule out the actuality of an incident simply because it corresponds, or can be interpreted to correspond, to a verse of scripture. But one may approach the question with an open mind, to ask which explanation is more likely.

The problem of eye-witnesses

The difficulty of a historical, as opposed to a theological, interpretation lies in the witnesses. In the synoptic account, while there is no sign that any of the disciples was present at the crucifixion, each individual episode *can* be accounted for on other grounds. In Mark's version the last appearance of a plausible source of information is Simon of Cyrene, 'the father of Alexander and Rufus', until the holy women are mentioned as 'looking on from a distance' in accordance with the scriptures. The only factor in his account which has not been shown to be fulfilment of the scriptures is the time scheme of crucifixion at the third hour, darkness from the sixth until the ninth hours; and these are so schematic as immediately to suggest some formal pattern. Matthew adds nothing which suggests a separate source of information: he alters the wording a little, accommodating it in several places to his characteristic vocabulary and mode of expression, clarifies some scriptural references, adds the earthquake and the foretaste of resurrection, and puts twice on the lips of Jesus's taunters the gibe that he claimed to be Son of God—a title on which Matthew lays especial emphasis, and which he inserts several times in his gospel. Matthew, then, does not suggest any additional eye-witness. Luke does have two considerable additions, but they correspond so perfectly with the particular interest of his tradition that one still wonders whether they are the result of additional information or only embroidery of Mark's version. The first major difference occurs already on the way to Golgotha: Luke omits here the offer of a narcotic drink; presumably he considers that it doubles up with the drink offered to him on the cross (both are fulfilments of the same verse of scripture) for, careful historian that he is, he often omits what could be considered a second version of the same incident. Instead, Jesus turns to the women who are following him, full of repentance (a Lukan theme), and makes a prophecy to them which could have been taken from sayings similar to those which compose the eschato-logical discourse in Lk 21. The second major difference we have already mentioned, the elaboration on the good thief, which betrays several Lukan elements. Apart from these Luke's only two notable changes are a different interpretation of Jesus's last cry, a psalm-verse emphasis-ing Jesus's acceptance of the Father's will, and the general conversion of the onlookers at Jesus's death, preparing for the conversions ·of the Acts of the Apostles. There is, then, no incontrovertible *need* to posit witnesses as the source of the incidents told by the synoptics. In themselves they could be the result of intensive and prolonged reflection on the event of the cross and its significance in terms of the bible.

When we come to John the situation is less clear-cut. One immediate difficulty is that John has no mention of a large number of details and even of incidents mentioned by the synoptics, even though some of them would have served his theological purposes admirably (eg the darkness over the earth in function of his theme of light, cf Jn 13:30). Even where he has basically the same incident, the details are often different, eg in the case of the division of clothes. A simple solution would be to give John the preference in each case, on the grounds that he receives his information from the beloved disciple who was actually present; but this solution itself labours under the difficulty of being contradictory to the synoptics, according to whom all the disciples fled at Jesus's arrest, and who do not number Mary the mother of Jesus even among the women who were looking on from afar. Raymond Brown, to whose stimulating commentary *(The Gospel according to St John,* London 1971) the present writer is much indebted, considers that 'Mary was specifically mentioned in the tradition which came to the evangelist . . . but that the reference to the Beloved Disciple, here as elsewhere, is a supplement to the tradition' yet that 'that addition is not necessarily unhistorical' (p 922). He refuses to pronounce on the question of the historicity of the episode, which is the centre of John's presentation of the crucifixion scene and his main point of difference from the synoptics. The important point is its significance: Mary is the new Eve, giving birth to the church by becoming the mother of the beloved disciple, who here stands for the whole community of believers. It is remarkable that according to this interpretation, especially when coupled to the incident of the piercing of Christ's side which we have already discussed, the fourth gospel rejoins by a different way the teaching of the synoptic evangelists that the death of Jesus is the moment of the foundation of the church.

It is often considered that, while the fourth gospel incorporates methods such as symbolism into historical narratives to bring out the meaning of the event, the synoptic gospels present a straightforward and soberly factual account. The present investigation has shown that, at a point at which the two traditions are closest together, the difference between them lies not so much in the extent as in the emphasis of their interpretation. Mark, in what must be closest to the primitive pre-gospel tradition, concentrates on showing that Jesus's crucifixion fulfils the Father's will perfectly by corresponding in every detail to this will as expressed in God's word in the old testament. Apart from this he does no more than briefly indicate the cosmic dimensions of the event — an aspect underlined by Matthew — and the entry of the gentiles into the community of believers at the death of Jesus. Matthew makes little significant change in Mark's account, but Luke, typically of what has been called the gospel of repentance and conversion, underlines the repentance and conversion of groups and individuals at this climax of Jesus's mission, with Jesus showing them the mercy which is especially characteristic of the Lukan Christ. John, on the other hand, regards the crucifixion first and foremost as the moment of the founding of the church, for to this are related several of the incidents which he tells. Such are the variations in emphasis of interpretation in the traditions which the evangelists incorporate in their gospels; each relates the same event, but each with its own particular view of its theological significance expressed by the narrative itself.

11

The resurrection

I

As one might expect of the event which above all others is central to the christian faith, theological discussion of the resurrection serves to focus the issues in at least two areas of biblical theology which have been major battlefields in recent years. On the one hand, it is the area where Bultmannian thought reaches the point where it must either transform the believer's whole attitude to the events of the gospel or be rejected as not ultimately satisfying the needs of faith. This controversy is, on the whole, between the liberal protestant attitude and the catholic-minded, though some members of the catholic communion will sometimes be found to be straying — bewilderment or determination in their eyes — considerably nearer the enemy lines than their senior officers would expect. On the other hand, the gospel narratives of the resurrection provide the perfect bone of contention between the older school of exegetes, who insist on the historical exactitude of the gospels, and the newer school, which holds that the evangelists sit far more lightly to detailed factual accuracy of reporting, and centre their interest on theological interpretation. This controversy is fought out (if that is the correct description of a situation in which each side

merely holds its ground and asserts the error of the
other, with barely any interchange or alteration of
position) far more within the bastion of orthodoxy
itself.

Demythologisation of the resurrection

The large-scale application in recent years of Bultmann's
general exegetical and theological principles to the
resurrection seems to date from a statement which he
made in a lecture at Heidelberg in 1960: 'To believe in
the Christ present in the kerygma is the meaning of the
Easter faith' (Quoted in Moule, C. D. F. *Significance of
the Message of the Resurrection,* London, 1967, p 18).
This position was not, of course, new. In *Kerygma and
Myth,* he had written: 'The faith of Easter is just this -
faith in the Word of preaching' (Ed H. W. Bartsch,
translated by R. H. Fuller, London, 1953, p 41.) To
Bultmann, investigation into the Christ of history is no
more than a means to the encounter with Christ in the
present; it is quite irrelevant whether any bodily
resurrection happened or not. It could not in fact have
happened, though he will concede that a 'series of
subjective visions' may have occurred. But in any case,
'objective investigation can lead only to the Christ of
Historie; it is totally unable to reach the Christ of
Geschichte' (Owen, H. P.: *Revelation and Existence, a
study in the theology of R. Bultmann,* Cardiff, 1957, p
28. In his clear analysis, the author defines *Historie* as of
what is wholly in the past and so dead, while *Geschichte*
is concerned with what 'both lies in the past and has
existential significance for the present', p 25. Faith is

concerned, then, only with the Christ of *Geschichte*.)

The Bultmannian approach to the resurrection was developed in a highly controversial series of lectures given at Münster in 1967/8 by Willi Marxsen. The presupposition behind his investigation is that the more our faith is a for it must be founded on experience of Christ now, not relying on the irrelevancies of *Historie*. Faith must be a miracle, and faith which relies on the evidence of signs and wonders is precisely a barrier to real faith (*The Resurrection of Jesus of Nazareth*, London, 1970, p 153). Since the evangelists could not therefore have intended to provide us with evidence of signs and wonders, and thus lead us into the mistake of relying on them, the gospel accounts of the resurrection appearances are so many protestations of faith and of experience of Jesus; the evangelists are, in the enthusiastic sense, testifying, witnessing to their experience of the risen Christ. And to express this experience of Christ today as 'Jesus is risen' is only one of many possible expressions of the christian hope for the future, merely using myth to express what could also - though less colourfully and so less effectively - be conveyed by 'still he comes today' (p 141); or even without any explicit reference to Christ, in the words of Heinrich Rendtorff on his deathbed, 'I shall be safe' (p 188). Even in the new testament, the statement of belief in Jesus' resurrection is only one possible way among many of expressing faith. In the letter to the Hebrews the idea does not occur at all, being replaced by that of exaltation, sitting down at the right hand of God: this is also the central concept of the very early hymn enshrined in Philippians (2: 5-11). In Matthew we find side by side, providing two originally independent and self-sufficient statements of belief, the story of the empty tomb and the saying, 'All authority in heaven and on earth has been given to me' (28: 18). In early Paul it is the expectation that Christ will soon come again which is uppermost; in John the notion of a saving transformation which has already occurred through Christ.

In Marxsen's scheme of things it is essentially faith which comes first, and the genesis of the centrality of the resurrection is outlined thus:

> Someone discovers in a miraculous way that Jesus evokes faith even after his death. He now asks what makes it possible for him to find faith in this way. The reason is that the Jesus who died is alive. He did not remain among the dead. But if one wanted to claim that a dead person was alive, then the notion of the resurrection of the dead was ready to hand. So one made use of it. In so doing there was no need to pin oneself down to a particular form of this idea, at least not at the beginning . . . If the idea of the resurrection eventually won the ascendancy, towing the other ideas in its wake, it must not be forgotten that it was a later development (pp 138, 147).

In what might well have been a commentary on this statement, Moule, in the introduction to the book he edited on the resurrection, remarks that it is not really sufficient to say that the idea of the resurrection of the dead was ready to hand, for the pharisees envisaged the permanent raising to unending life only in the general resurrection at the *eschaton* (though they knew of miraculous returns to this life, such as that worked by Elijah on the widow of Zarephtah's son (1 Kg 17: 17 ff). But the fundamental cleavage, as he points out, is between those who say that the resurrection is the expression of an already existing faith, and those who say it is the cause. In the former category fall Marxsen and Bultmann. Perhaps worth quoting as an extreme form of this position, garish in its popularity, is that of J. A. T. Robinson, who describes the resurrection experience thus:

> And then IT happened. It came to them — or rather, as they could only describe it, HE came to them. The life they had known and shared was not buried with him but alive in them. Jesus was not a dead memory but a living presence . . . But the empty tomb is not the resurrection any more than the shell of the cocoon is the butterfly . . . Precisely what happened to the body we shall never know. (*But That I Can't Believe,* London, 1967, pp 37-40.)

In all this there are clearly several issues at stake. The first is that of the nature of faith and the part played in its genesis by various elements, particularly the motives of credibility and the unaccountable experience which transforms the willingness to believe into belief itself. For the followers of Bultmann, as for many brands of revivalist preacher, faith is a sudden and inexplicable seizing-hold-of, like the rushing down of the Spirit of God in the old testament upon judges and prophets. Little or no psychological preparation is required, and accordingly the motives of credibility lose their importance. It may be — though I doubt it, even for the United States with their striking recrudescence of devotion to the Spirit — that a majority of people reach faith in the first place through this experience rather than through learning about God and the Jesus of the gospels. But at least later the motives of credibility must surely play their part. (*Epiphanie als Geschichte,* Munich,1966, and discussion in *Orientierung* of 15 May, 1967, pp 108-112).

A second issue is that of *Historie* and *Geschichte.* It seems to me that a basic logical fallacy, of the type pilloried by Lewis Carroll in *Through the Looking Glass,* is involved here. It is practically a claim of smoke without fire. If the christian hope has any reference to the Christ of *Geschichte,* if the conviction that 'I shall be safe' has any dependence on him, there must be some reason for his position. The Christ of *Geschichte* would not be what he is, were it not for the factual history of two thousand years ago. When Bultmann qualifies this as *Historie,* he is simply using the word as a value word to make a value-judgment. Of course, *if* the events in Palestine at this time are *Historie,* they are dead history; but it is mere sleight of hand to define them as *Historie* and then claim them to be dead history. This is surely the whole issue at stake. One can just as well claim that the events were vitally important for the significance of Jesus today.

Quite another question is whether and to what extent the events are described in a mythical fashion. Myth is 'the use of imagery to express the other-worldly in terms of this world, and the divine in terms of human life, the other side in terms of this side. For instance, divine transcendence is expressed as spatial distance' (Bultmann, *Kerygma and Myth,* p 10, note 2). Now it is surely acceptable to all that some mythological terms must be used to describe the other-worldly, whether these be 'Son of Man', with reference to Daniel's vision, or 'Jesus Christ, superstar', with reference to a more modern mythology. But to say that an event is described mythologically is only to say that the significance of the event is being written into the description of the event, and is quite different from saying that the event itself is a mere myth or did not happen. Different mythologies can be used to describe the same event, and the use of several, such as resurrection, exaltation at the right hand of God, expectation of a coming in power, to describe the event which is the foundation of the christian hope does not mean that no such event occurred. Nor, for that matter, is Marxsen justified in claiming that the mythology of 'resurrection' was 'a later development'. The telling of the story of the empty tomb may be later (which is no proof that the story itself is later, though it does suggest that less importance was attached to it at first). But although he can quote other formulations as occurring in pre-pauline hymns incorporated in Paul's letters, he omits to mention that the terminology of 'resurrection' also occurs in first Corinthians (1 Cor 15) as belonging to an ancient credal formula which was already part of the tradition memorised by converts.

A third issue will be dealt with at greater length later. It is the fundamental one: did the evangelists really think that they were only expressing their faith in the present power of Jesus, or did they consider that in presenting the accounts of the resurrection appearances they were presenting the events which were the basis and foundation of their faith? It is surely crucial that our faith should be in continuity with theirs and that we should discern and follow their intentions.

And the bones of Jesus?

Before going on to what must be the central point of our investigation, the testing of theories against the ultimate criterion of the gospel texts, we must examine the further point, what must have happened to Jesus' body? At one level this can be investigated with the gospels as the point of departure. At another level, it is important to investigate the importance itself of this point, for it has been widely asserted that it would make no difference to faith if the bones of Jesus were one day to be found in Palestine (eg Neville Clarke, in *Significance of the Message of the Resurrection,* p 97). At first sight this assertion is stunning, the direct contradiction of the naive view of the resurrection. But the position changes when one considers that Jesus did not come *back* to life but rose to new life. There is a vast difference between the resurrection of Lazarus, who rose from the dead to the same sort of bodily existence and presumably died later, and Christ's resurrection to a new and transformed life. The details of this transformation of the life-principle are less important here, (see the present writer's article in *Clergy Review,* 53, 1968, pp 251-8) but clearly his life was not subject to the normal limitations of human life, nor was his bodily movement so restricted, nor does he seem to have been subject to the normal requirements of nourishment. He had, indeed, a body; but what is a 'spiritual' body? Must it be in continuity with the body of flesh which precedes the resurrection? If so, in what sense are our bodies going to be in continuity, when all the molecules of our bodies have been used for other purposes? Some molecules must have gone to compose several people.

Are there, indeed, enough molecules to go round all the people who will have to rise again? If the risen body has no molecules, in what sense is it a body? What precisely is meant by the resurrection of *the body*? In any case, some sort of answer must be given to these questions before it is assumed *a priori* — that is, apart from the gospel accounts — that Jesus's body must have been removed by God from the tomb for him to have risen to new life.

The theological arguments in this matter are difficult to evaluate. In the interesting dialogue between Professors Lampe and MacKinnon (G. W. H. Lampe and D. M. MacKinnon, *The Resurrection,* London, 1966) the former, though maintaining the reality of the resurrection appearances, does not consider the tomb to be empty. Paul, at any rate, he maintains, did not know about the story; the argument from silence is very strong: the story of the empty tomb would have strengthened Paul's arguments about the physical reality of the resurrection in 1 Cor 15. Further, argues Lampe, Paul's analogy with what he considers to happen in the case of the germination of a grain of wheat: 'the thing that you sow is not what is going to come; you sow a bare grain, say of wheat or something like that, and then God gives it the sort of body that he has chosen' (1Cor 15:37), excludes the idea of the spiritual body being in flesh-and-blood continuity with the earthly body. But here Professor Lampe is, I think, trying to press Paul to a clear answer where he can in fact only stutter in bewilderment and wonder. What Paul seems to be trying to express is that there is an analogy and some sort of continuity between the body now and the spiritual body of the resurrection. There is similarity and difference between the various sorts of 'fleshes' which he mentions, the 'flesh' of men, beasts, birds and fish, and the same is true of the brightnesses of sun, moon and stars; perhaps the best term for these is analogical similarity. The continuity can be deduced from 'whatever you sow in the ground has to die before it can be given new life' (1 Cor 15:36): the 'it' remains constant. But how far this continuity reaches and in what it consists does not seem to me at all clear in Paul's mind.

Paul is concerned chiefly with the quality of the risen body of the christian, not with that of Christ himself; though what he says of the christian of course applies also to Christ, since the risen Christ is the first-fruits and model of the risen christian. He details four attributes of the risen body: it is imperishable, powerful, spiritual and glorious. All these combine to mean that the risen body is somehow transformed by God and brought into closer union with God, transferred, as it were, into the sphere of the divine. For all these attributes are true primarily of God himself. In the Book of Wisdom, where first such thoughts are voiced, imperishability belongs to God alone, and is his prerogative. Similarly, 'spiritual' means for Paul 'caught up into God', for actions are spiritual just in so far as they are under the influence of the Spirit of God (in Paul's healthy anthropology, 'spiritual' has no over-tones of 'soulful' or of a tenuously physical substance, but is uniquely related to the Spirit of God). Where the Spirit of God is, there inevitably is the third attribute, power; for the Spirit, from the first mention of its being given to men, is something which gives them power to carry out a task given by God; so, in the christian life on earth, it gives power to live as sons of God. Finally, glory is most clearly of all the prerogative of God; it has nothing to do with worldly reputation or fame, but is the awesome quality which belongs to God in the highest heavens. But Paul cannot make clear — or at least he does not — where the old physical qualities of the earthly body fit in.

More daunting is Professor Lampe's contention that if the tomb was empty, Christ's resurrection is not the pledge of ours. Our bodies corrupt before resurrection, and it would seem that if the tomb was empty Christ's did not. But even this is not acceptable; though the reason for its being unacceptable does not ease any difficulties for the advocates of any sort of bodily resurrection. The naive theory that Jesus died but his body did not corrupt would be regarded nowadays as a contradiction in terms. Corruption is the medical criterion of death, irreversible damage to the brain-cells, by which their structure changes (corrupts) within two minutes of the cessation of the flow of blood to the brain. If there is not this corruption then we have a case of suspended animation rather than true death. If Jesus really died, then his body really corrupted. Was this process miraculously nullified at the resurrection or does corruption of the flesh-and-blood body not attaint the spiritual body of the resurrection? In either case Lampe's argument is not cogent for, no less than ours, Jesus' body corrupted before his resurrection.

Advances in chemistry and biology since the dawn of the scientific era have made it difficult to say much about the risen body. Further, one must query the limitations of Paul's anthropology. It is primarily the person who rises again; the doctrine of the resurrection of the body is formulated to stress that it is the whole person who rises, not just a neo-platonic soul. This is an emphasis congenial both to Paul's semitic anthropology of the whole man, according to which it is impossible to envisage a disembodied soul on the platonic sense, and to modern thought. But the formidable problems of space and matter involved raise the question, in what sense the body can be said to rise again. (Cf also K. Rahner, *On the Theology of Death,* London, 1961.) And in this case the same problem applies to Christ, 'the first born from the dead' (Col 1:18) or the 'first-fruits' of the resurrection (1 Cor 15:23). In the present state of knowledge, then, it does not seem to me possible to say that if the bones of Jesus were one day to be found in Palestine one would have to conclude that the resurrection was not a historical event, that the resurrection appearances were not objective occurrences. Relevant here are the remarks of Michael Simpson SJ (*Death and Eternal Life,* Dublin, 1971, pp 60-65) on symbolic and non-symbolic language. If we press symbolic language too far, or treat it as non-symbolic, we miss the meaning and reach only confusion.

It remains to examine the gospel and other new testament texts on the resurrection and the resurrection appearances. We must discover what the evangelists considered to have happened, and how they interpreted the events.

II

Presuppositions

It is impossible to undertake an enquiry of this kind

without prior acceptance of a method. In the method which I propose to adopt, there are two elements with which some readers may disagree, and which had therefore better be clearly stated at the outset. To justify them fully would require volumes on their own, but here no more than a *rationale* can be sketched.

The first presupposition is that the evangelists are primarily christian teachers engaged in mediating the christian message. The christian message, like the Jewish before it, is essentially grounded on historical events, but this does not make the evangelists historians — or at least not in the narrow sense of chroniclers, though we might call them historians of the good news of Christ (cf John L. McKenzie's excellent remarks on 'History', in his *Dictionary of the Bible*, London, 1965, p 360; and Xavier Léon-Dufour, *The Gospels and the Jesus of History*, London, 1968, pp 28-30). Furthermore, the material which they pass on to us they had themselves received from the early communities, where it had been preserved and handed on because of its message. While it is naive and unfounded to maintain, as some do, that the early communities had their sights so firmly fixed on the fast approaching end of the world that they had no interest in history, it is equally false to insist that their interest in Christ's words and deeds was as keen historically as it was doctrinally. Since the communities were concerned with the stories of Jesus more for their message to christians than for their historical exactitude, we may expect that in their transmission, as in the telling of any story, the stories were adjusted to bring out to the maximum the message they contained, even at the price of factual exactitude. For example, if I say, in the course of a story, that a man 'drew himself up to his full height', it would be quite irrelevant to object that a man cannot change his height. I am not talking about his height, but about the manner and emphasis of his reply — with his full dignity, measured tones, etc. One could object that my expression was historically inexact — and one would have missed my point. Anyone who wishes to bring out the point of an episode or series of episodes will select, compress or expand, change a phrase here and there, in order to make the speaker's meaning more obvious to the narrator's audience. He may, legitimately, even put words into his subject's mouth, to express succinctly and dramatically what would otherwise have required a flat and laborious explanation. These are the accepted norms of any storyteller, and we should not expect the gospel writers to have been preserved from (or deprived of) them.

The second presupposition is that Matthew and Luke use two sources of information, Mark and a collection of sayings of the Lord usually known as Q (cf Grant, F. C.: *The Gospels, their origin and their growth,* London, 1957, esp pp 44 ff: the latter source does not concern us because it was not used in the passages under discussion). What in Matthew and Luke does not derive from these two sources is the result of their own editing. Each evangelist, like every christian, saw certain aspects of Christ and his message to be of paramount importance; and each, in his desire to teach the essential message of Christ, stressed particular aspects. It is this difference of emphasis, rather than different sources of information, which explains the minor variations in telling a story between Matthew and Luke (eg the centurion of Capernaum, Mt 8:5 ff; Lk 7:1 ff). But consideration of the relationship between the gospels as a whole does exclude the possibility of Matthew and Luke having any other source of factual information which they used to cross-check or expand the narratives they received from Mark. Whether they had any narrative source about Jesus for the stories and, for example, the parables which they relate independently of Mark and Q, is more doubtful. It would certainly be strange if this source included only incidents omitted by Mark, or if they failed to use such a source because they had Mark as a source. A large number of incidents and parables can be explained by the Jewish technique of midrash (a wide term, which includes the description of events by means of biblical references and allusions to past biblical events, in order to bring out their significance — cf McKenzie's *Dictionary of the Bible* sv). Matthew certainly uses this, for instance in the infancy narratives, and in recounting the death of Judas. Luke, for his part, has a recognisable predilection for presenting theological lessons in the form of a story (this is particularly clear in the Acts of the Apostles, eg in the story of Pentecost). In some cases, the point of departure for the development can be clearly perceived. In any case, there are a number of instances where a story which is proper to Matthew or Luke is clearly elaborated by them without previous factual source.

A third presupposition must also be mentioned: that Mark's gospel originally ended at 16:8. Although this is now generally accepted, it perhaps requires some explanation. The three alternative endings after that verse offered by various manuscripts are all unsatisfactory: the one for which there is most manuscript evidence is the longest; and this ending diverges very clearly from Mark's style and method, being in fact a concatenation of texts found elsewhere in the gospels and Acts. All three are the product of the feeling, derived by comparison with the other gospels, that there must have been something after verse 8. But firstly, it is difficult to envisage how this ending disappeared without leaving a trace in any manuscript or tradition. Secondly, if one prescinds from the other gospels (which did not exist when Mark wrote), the ending seems perfectly satisfactory and complete at verse 8: the crucifixion story is happily concluded with the angel's declaration of the resurrection. The gospel terminates on the beautifully open-ended and mysterious note of the awe of the women, which at the same time closes the incident because they do not give the message.

Matthew's view of the risen Lord

It was emphasised in the previous section that we can arrive at the truth about Jesus only through the evangelists. If they are wrong, we are lost. It is therefore of the first importance to discover their view of the resurrection rather than putting to them questions which cut across their train of thought. Matthew is the most straightforward of them, because his account points single-mindedly to the final incident on the mountain in Galilee. He makes some other minor changes in adopting Mark's narrative about the empty tomb, but the most noticeable is the speeding towards Galilee: the women in Matthew are to 'go quickly' (28:7) to deliver the message to the apostles, which has a double, emphatic 'and behold' added (almost 'look here'). Far from being silenced by awe, they 'ran off' to

tell the disciples, only to have their resolution strengthened by a vision of Jesus himself, who does no more
than reinforce the same commission. Everything in
Matthew, then, is hastening towards the mountain-top
in Galilee.

At the same time Matthew does, of course, insist on
the emptiness of the tomb with his story of the guards.
He also insists that something supernatural happened,
some divine intervention. This is the meaning of the
earthquake which he inserts here, following the well-
attested old testament and Jewish convention of
describing a divine visitation by means of cosmic
disturbances. So, as well as interpreting the meaning of
the resurrection existentially, he also insists on its
physical reality.

An existential interpretation is the purpose of the last
paragraph of the gospel. It is clearly the composition of
the evangelist himself, for it contains a very high
proportion of words and expressions used by Matthew
alone of the evangelists (at least seven in the four
verses). In addition many other expressions used in the
paragraph are characteristic of his style (cf Kilpatrick,
G, D.: *The Origins of the Gospel according to St
Matthew*, Oxford, 1946, pp 48 ff), so that it is
indisputable that at least the bare bones of the story
were composed by the evangelist. The two dominant
themes — and so the substance of what Matthew wants
to teach about the risen Lord — are the exaltation of
Christ and the consequent missionary charge and
promise. The two themes are interwoven, and exegetes
vary about where the emphasis falls; but certainly it is in
virtue of his exaltation, described in terms of Daniel's
vision (Dan 7:13 ff), 'All authority in heaven and on

earth has been given to me', that Christ sends his
disciples on their universal mission and promises to be
present always to his church. This theme is a fitting
climax to Matthew's gospel, arching over as it does from
the first chapter, where the interpretation of Emmanuel,
'God with us', has an important place. And it is picked
up again in the chapter on the community, 'Where two
or three meet in my name, I shall be there with them'
(Mt 18:20), and by the frequent promise that what is
done to missionaries or disciples of Christ is done also to
him (Lk 9:48; 10:16).

As far as Matthew is concerned, then, the existential
interpretation proposed by the Bultmann school, 'Still
he comes today' (cf p 109), does have a lot to
recommend it. It brings out the double aspect of the
power and presence of Christ now in his church; this is
indeed Matthew's final message. But there are two
elements which we find to be lacking. One of these is
the warrant of this presence, and the guarantee of its
effectiveness which is given precisely by the mythological overtones of the reference to Daniel's vision of
the Son of Man. When one is speaking of a situation
which lies outside and above the realms of our normal
everyday, humdrum experience, one must use some sort
of symbolism. To fail to take this for what it is, is as
short-sighted as the failure to understand poetic
language as poetry. This language expresses something
which is really there (just as poetry may express
something about a situation which cannot be contained
by prose). Granted that this language is symbolic rather
than literal, there is nevertheless something real expressed symbolically by these assertions about Christ's
position as Lord of the universe. The other element

stressed by Matthew which is lacking in the Bultmann approach is the empty tomb; to this we shall return.

The risen Lord according to Luke

Different as are Luke's post-resurrection stories from those of Matthew, there is yet a remarkable similarity in their teaching. One feels that when he wrote them, Luke already had the Acts of the Apostles in mind. If any theme is prominent in the Acts, it is missionary preaching, and this is the theme stressed by Luke's narratives.

He also makes quite deliberately a highly significant geographical adjustment. His stories are all in or around Jerusalem, in accordance with his scheme which makes Jerusalem pivotal in the gospel. The later part of his gospel, from 9:51 onwards, is the journey up to Jerusalem, where Jesus must accomplish his death (all other place-names are rigorously excluded to avoid distraction). Similarly, the pattern of Acts is the gradual spread of the gospel in ever-widening circles out from Jerusalem. This is perhaps one way in which Luke expresses the importance of charity and church unity: the churches remain always careful of their unity with the mother-church of Jerusalem. Perhaps it is also another way of stressing the pivotal nature of Christ's death and resurrection which made Jerusalem the centre of the church. But possibly more significant than the theology behind the change is the way in which the change itself is operated. In Mark he read: 'He will go before you *into Galilee;* there you will see him *as he said to you*' (16:7 referring to the promise made in

Gethsemane — Mk 14:28). Luke must have been aware
that there were traditions of appearance in Galilee
which fulfilled this promise; they are recorded in
Matthew and John (Mt 28:16ff; Jn 21). Yet in order to
ignore them, Luke changes the angel's words to
'Remember what *he said to you* when he was still *in
Galilee*' (24:6): omitting the promise made in
Gethsemane, yet providing no corresponding saying
during the Galilaean ministry. If history is no more than
the exact recording of the minutiae of events, this can
only be described as deliberate falsification of history.
Such treatment shows, however, that it is not in the
details of historical circumstance but in the salvific
content of the lesson of events that the interest of the
evangelist lies. If the evangelists can be described as
historians at all, it is as historians of a person and of his
message; it is their business to convey a faithful record
of his whole personality, rather than of each event for
itself. And an attempt to splice the narratives of the
different gospels into a single smooth-running newsreel
is not the task of one who wishes to come nearer to the
mind of the writers.

As we have said, Luke views the resurrection
primarily as the starting-point of the christian mission.
Missionary preaching begins already with the angels of
the resurrection, whose purpose is to interpret the
event. (Why does he change Mark's single angel into
two? Is it fanciful to connect this with the sending out
of the disciples on their mission in pairs, Lk 10:1?)
Their message is already couched in terms which will
become familiar in the missionary discourses of the Acts
(Lk 24:7; cf Acts 2:23-24; 3:13-15; 13:30 etc). Even
more striking is the example of missionary preaching

given by the risen Lord himself, which forms the centre-piece of the journey to Emmaus (Lk 24:13-31). Here the risen Christ instructs the two disciples with much the same method, proof from scripture, as is used in the Acts, and often in the same words. Particularly clear is the parallel with Philip's evangelisation of the courtier in Acts (8:26-40). And as in the Acts preaching leads on to a sacrament, so here; only in the Acts it leads on to baptism, which would be inappropriate for those who are already disciples and who therefore join the Lord in the eucharist. Thus the risen Lord is for Luke the model of the christian preacher.

The last two paragraphs of the gospel are also unmistakably a preparation for the life of the church as described in the Acts. Jesus this time teaches the assembled disciples, again in the same style and language, before sending them out as his representatives to do the same. And finally he departs, leaving them with a solemn blessing for their task.

Luke therefore, like Matthew, is not content merely to sit back and wonder at the risen Lord. The resurrection is not just an event which happened in the past. They insist that the risen Lord has a permanent message. This Matthew expresses by the command to make disciples and baptise, in the strength of the promise of continual presence given by him who holds all power in heaven and on earth. Luke expresses the same missionary concern by means of the triple model of the apostolic kerygma and the final command and blessing. In both cases it is the lasting influence and active power of the risen Lord in his church that comes to the fore: 'Still he comes today'.

But in Luke, just as in Matthew, there is also the

stress on the bodily reality of the resurrection. Matthew stresses the emptiness of the tomb by his story of the guards: a polemic against those who claimed that his body had been stolen. Luke answers a different charge, that it was not a real, physical body. This is the point of Jesus' showing his hands and his feet and being given something to eat, with the explicit mention that he ate the piece of fish 'before their eyes'.

The message of Mark

Of the synoptic writers, Mark is the most primitive and the simplest. As his one episode is shared by the more fully developed evangelists, it has been convenient to defer its discussion till now, after the tendencies of the others have been examined. The story of the empty tomb is of course the rock of scandal for those who would hold that the stories of the risen Christ are the result of an already-existing faith in his presence now, rather than the cause of it. Indeed we have seen that the main drive of the other stories is to explain the mode and effect of the presence in the church of the risen Christ. That the message is given by means of these stories could indeed be a poetical way of teaching such truths, resulting from a conviction of his presence, But the Bultmann theory of 'a series of subjective visions' is brought up short against the story of the empty tomb: a story which, moreover, determines the modality of all the others. If the early christians had not been convinced of its truth, they would have expressed these same lessons about the presence of Christ in the church, and his command to it, in a different way.

There are two ways of disposing of the story of the empty tomb which deserve notice. The first has already been mentioned; the idea of resurrection was 'a later development' (p 113). As we have already remarked, such a statement can be made only in bland disregard of the oldest credal formula we possess (1 Cor 15:4). Paul claims to have learnt this formula himself and taught it to his Corinthian converts, presumably as part of their elementary instruction, in the year 51-52 AD. This is, by quite a large margin, the earliest date we can give to any christian statement. What is, however, true is that Paul shows no awareness of the story of the empty tomb; so that the way is open for saying that the first basis, chronologically, for belief in the resurrection was the experience of the risen Lord appearing to the witnesses cited in first Corinthians. (But it should be noted that the appearances are bodily ones: he can be 'seen', a fact which is hardly stressed by the demythologising school.) But it is true only that the way is open; the conclusion does not impose itself. An alternative explanation for citing these witnesses to the risen Christ rather that telling the story of the empty tomb is that it would be both more convincing and more apt theologically. More apt theologically, because the empty tomb is of no account if the risen Christ does not make his presence felt, while the reverse is not true; more convincing, because the testimony of a few overwrought women is so patently weak. Bultmann and his followers seem to have no difficulty in simply writing the story off as legend: 'The stories of the empty tomb, of which Paul has no knowledge yet, are legends'. (Bultmann, R.: *Theologie des NT* Tübingen, 1965, p 48). 'The late origin of the pericope about the tomb is already suggested by its legendary character'. (Grass, H,: *Ostergeschehen und Osterberichte*, Göttingen, 1956, p 23). They base everything on Paul's silence, interpreting this to mean that he did not know the story, without considering the possibility that he deliberately passes it over because the witness of women has no validity in Jewish law; and because he can also prove his point by the testimony of the apostles, the authorised witnesses to the resurrection. Paradoxically, the very weakness of the story is an argument in favour of its basic historicity.

The second way of disposing of the story of the empty tomb is less crude, since it does at least set out to explain how the stories arose. To the total Jewish anthropology it was inconceivable that a person could have any non-bodily existence. But it was clear that Jesus continued to exist and act. Therefore he must have a body, which he could have in no other way than by resuming the body which lay in the tomb. The story of the empty tomb, and the stories of Jesus being touched and eating, are the result of this basically philosophical presupposition that non-bodily life is impossible. (Marxsen perhaps follows the same line of thought when he dismisses the evidence of the story thus: 'The message of the resurrection, which already exists as a formula, is therefore re-interpreted in visual terms' Marxsen, W.: *The Resurrection of Jesus of Nazareth*, London, 1970, p 161). It will be clear from the final paragraphs of the first section that modern science in no way rules out the possibility that Jesus *could* have had some sort of bodily existence even if his body had remained in the tomb. But is it so clear that the earliest christians could not have realised this? Is it so certain that they would have had to invent an empty tomb to explain their experience of a bodily risen Christ?

Two factors suffice to create at least uncertainty on this point. The earliest christians were well aware that Christ's body was not the same in all respects as it had been before his death. Not only could it pass through locked doors, but it was so altered as to be recognisable only with difficulty and that to the eyes of love (this trait emerges most clearly in John, both in the case of the Magdalen and of the apostle on the lake, but it can be perceived also in the story of the disciples at Emmaus). More especially, we may not wholly agree with Professor Lampe's view that Paul's arguments about the risen body exclude the continuity of the risen body with that of the earthly (p 115). Nevertheless the situation is not such that Paul would clearly have to invent a story of an empty tomb if he were to continue to hold the bodily resurrection of Christ. And if Paul would not need to, why should other early christians?

In any case, with the claim that the story of the empty tomb was invented later for apologetic reasons, in order to answer the charge that Christ was not really risen, we come to a parting of the ways. Confronted with such a story — or indeed with any other part of the gospel tradition — it is the automatic reaction of the Bultmann school to ask why this was written. This is particularly clear in the volume of essays *The Future of our Religious Past*, ed Robinson, J. M., London, 1971, esp chs 7 and 8. On the supposition that the gospel tradition was created to serve the needs of the preaching and teaching community, the hypothesis that the event actually occurred is entertained only as a remote (and rather irrelevant) possibility. This is an inevitable result of their presuppositions about faith being necessarily a leap in the dark, and the darker the better. Another school of exegesis would prefer — to put it at its weakest — to grant that there is a *prima facie* likelihood that there is at least some event behind a gospel story.

It is, of course, possible to hold that some stories were created by the evangelist on a very slender basis. It has frequently been suggested, for example, that some of the miracle stories in Matthew were composed in reliance on the generalised memory that Jesus was a wonder-worker (cf Fuller, R. H.: *Interpreting the Miracles,* London, 1963, p 86). Certainly—the comparison with Matthew makes it plain — Luke simply inserts without factual warrant miracles in connection with the messengers from John the Baptist (7:21) or rather transfers them to this occasion because of the general knowledge of Jesus' cures. Similarly, the story of the flight into Egypt is so clearly and minutely modelled on the infancy of Moses that it is far more likely that Matthew is working from the stories of Moses' infancy than from memories of that of Jesus (p 54).

But there is a clear difference of literary type and emphasis between these examples and the narrative of the empty tomb. In some cases, the core may be almost entirely scriptural, to show that Jesus is fulfilling the old testament by re-incarnating its great prophets: Moses in the flight into Egypt, Elijah and Elisha in the raising of the widow's son at Nain (Lk 7: 11ff). But in all cases there is some discernible basis on which the evangelist is building, other than the mere need for apologetic reasons to assert that it happened. It is a guess, unsubstantiated by solid parallels and therefore unscientific, to assert that the story is 'the message of the resurrection . . . interpreted in visual terms', 'the pro-clamation . . . is externalised in the reference to the empty tomb'. (Marxsen, *op cit,* pp 161, 163). A further difference is the uniqueness of this event. If it were proved that one or other of the miracle-stories were entirely invented, the message of the wonder-worker interpreted in visual terms, this would still be acceptable as the further repetition of a message already shown, adding nothing new. Yet another difference is the fact that this narrative is one of the very few that is given by all four evangelists, and accorded a central position. The differences between the synoptic accounts and John are signs of some elaboration; but they are, at the same time, proof of the strength of the tradition of the empty tomb and the appearance to women there.

To sum up, then, the arguments against the claim that the story of the empty tomb was invented for apolo-getic reasons. The earliest known christian credal formula shows the christians already believing in a visible risen Christ; nevertheless it is not clear that this would necessarily involve an empty tomb, so that it would not have been necessary to invent such a story. Secondly, as proof, the story is weak, for the testimony of women is invalid in Jewish law. If the christians were inventing a story to prove a point which was the key-stone of their message, they might have been expected to invent a better one. Thirdly, on a point of method, in spite of all the qualifications made about historical exactitude, at the beginning of this section strong evidence is required for the assertion that such a central story, common to all the gospels, is a complete fabrication, and not simply an interpreted version to which at least *some* event stands as factual basis and point of departure. Analyses of how some narratives have been elaborated from a core have been attempted with varying success; but here there is supposed to be no factual core.

The core of history which is preserved in all the versions is only the emptiness of the tomb; that is the basic and central assertion of the incident. About the circumstances there is wide divergence even between the synoptics: was it getting light or after sunrise (Matthew v Mark)? Was Salome there or not (Mark v Matthew)? Did they come to anoint the body or just to visit the tomb (Mark and Luke v Matthew)? Was there an earthquake (Matthew alone)? Was there one angel or two (Matthew and Mark v Luke)? Did the women deliver the message or not (Matthew v Mark and Luke)? Did Jesus himself appear (Matthew alone)? By scrutinising the differences and similarities between the evangelists, we can discover what they found central and how they set about interpreting it.

The message of Mark in this, his only post-resurrection story, has a fine simplicity. It is not apologetic, for there is no statement that the women — feeble witnesses in any case, as we have already pointed out — check the angel's words. The first stress is on the atmosphere of awe and reverence engendered by the whole affair, for this is the sense of their stunned fear which is their reaction to the angel and their final attitude. Mark wants to leave this final, mysterious impression ringing at the end of his gospel: the awful power of God is at work. The second stress is provided by the angel's message. The *angelus interpres* is a recognised convention of Jewish literature, in the later books of the old testament and in non-biblical writings as well as the new testament (eg the angels of the ascension); they are the bearers of the divine message, the interpreters of an otherwise puzzling state of affairs. We must regard the angel's message here as related directly to Jesus' prediction that he would go before them into Galilee (Mk 14: 28). In the garden of Gethsemane this promise occurs at the same time as, and in spite of, the prediction that the disciples, and in particular Peter, will desert the Lord during his passion. The announcement here, therefore, again with particular reference to Peter, conveys a certain reconciliation and forgiveness. The same is to be understood from the greeting 'Do not be afraid'; in the bible, this is always the greeting given to the favoured beneficiary of a divine vision. The message is, then, that in spite of the awe rightly caused by these supernatural happenings, the disciples are the favoured friends of the risen Lord, and are to rejoin him in his power and mission.

Even in this short account of Mark, therefore, the story of the resurrection is no mere *Historie* but is *Geschichte,* fraught with existential import. Here again the message for the church of today is carried by the events of the past, not merely by the faith of the first christians. It was the events which gave rise to the faith, not the faith to the stories.

III

We now turn to the attitude to the resurrection taken up by John's gospel. Immediately striking about this are the much greater variety of the accounts in John, and the discreet but unmistakable angle of vision of the later church.

The variety of the stories and their relationship to those of the synoptics raises in acute form the question of the origin of all the resurrection accounts. C. H. Dodd some time ago classified all the gospel narratives about the resurrection into two basic categories, concise narratives (an appearance of Jesus, a recognition and a mission-charge by Jesus, eg the appearance on the mountain with which Matthew concludes), circum-stantial narratives (dramatic stories, much more developed than the former, such as the story of the disciples on the road to Emmaus) and — inevitably — some mixed forms ('The Appearances of the Risen Christ' in *Studies in the Gospel* ed D. R. Nineham, Oxford, 1955). This classification is not entirely satis-factory, nor is it clear what conclusions may be drawn from it, but it does suggest a useful simplification: if there are indeed two basic types this may give us the two basic forms of the tradition. In his recent and indispensable commentary Raymund E. Brown is more radical: 'A more biblical approach [than harmonisation] is to suppose that one basic appearance underlies all the main Gospel accounts of appearences to the Twelve (Eleven)' (*The Gospel according to John,* London 1971, p 972). He points out that since these appearances all lead up to a commission to preach, baptise, etc (with the exception of Jn 21:1-14, which he decisively separates from the command to Peter to 'feed my lambs') 'it makes little sense to construct a series of such appearances to the Twelve; each Gospel witness is reporting a slightly different version of an appearance that was constitutive of the Christian community' (p

973). The variety which exists between the different versions stems from their development within different communities and different traditions, shaped by different theological emphases and different imagery. Thus Luke suggests that the sole appearance to the Twelve was on the day of resurrection, and that this appearance culminated in the final blessing and parting on the road to Bethany (the prescence of the story of the disciples on the way to Emmaus makes this very awkward, since evening is already coming on when they begin their meal at Emmaus, seven miles from Jerusalem, and dusk falls fast in Palestine). John 20 splits the appearance into two in order to introduce the Thomas episode—a mixed narrative, since it has no mission charge—which enables him to stress two lessons about faith which are of the highest importance in his gospel, and also forms an excellent dramatic setting for the final confession of faith with which the gospel concludes (assuming as almost all now do that the gospel originally ended at ch 20). John 21 presents the appearance in a totally different context; it may even combine the memories of three distinct scenes: the first (21: 1-8) an appearance of Christ on the lake-shore and a catch of fish, the second (21: 9-13) a meal with the risen Christ, and the third the scene of promises to Peter and finally predictions about the future of the beloved disciple. The situation is complicated even more by the fact that each of these scenes has a certain similarity with gospel scenes of events during Jesus' earthly life: the first with the vocation to be fishers of men (Lk 5: 1-11), the second with the multiplication of the loaves and fishes, and the third with the promises to Peter made at Caesarea Philippi (Mt 16: 16-18). One is tempted to wonder whether the writer of the appendix has not taken elements from all these scenes and blended them together to create a conclusion which will enshrine important lessons for the future of the church.

The risen Christ and his disciple

If this view of the fluidity of the tradition and the multiplicity of its forms is justified, then there is all the more reason to concentrate on the message which the evangelist uses his narrative to convey. One of the most striking features of John's account is the beloved disciple, whose presence seems in a way to pervade the whole presentation. It has often been suggested that in the gospel of John Mary is both individual and a symbolic figure, standing for the church, of which she is the mother and the perfect exemplar. In the same way it is a most attractive suggestion that the curiously anonymous 'disciple whom Jesus loved' is also an exemplary and symbolic figure, standing for 'a disciple whom Jesus loves', in the collective sense of any faithful disciple in the future. Many solutions have been offered for the strange silence about his identity, the most common being that it is the author of the gospel, who refrains from mentioning his own name out of humility — an odd humility, since the silence about the name is combined with a stress on his special relationship with the Lord. Altogether more meaningful is to discard all idea of a half-hearted disguise and to accept the namelessness of the disciple as an indication that his personal identity is deliberately suppressed by the evangelist so that his significance may lie precisely in his faceless quality and the generality that it brings.

It is perhaps his role in the resurrection stories that is all-important, but this is prepared by his previous appearances. At the supper he is characterised by his intimacy with Jesus and the bond of affection which binds him to the Lord, making him the recipient of his secret revelation. In the courtyard of the high priest's house he is seen as — in contrast to the other disciples — faithful to Jesus in his passion, following his Lord in his sufferings where even Peter denies him. Finally he alone remains at the foot of the cross, there standing over against the figure of Mary, the mother of the church. If, as has frequently been suggested, Mary here corresponds to the daughter of Sion, the mother of God's chosen people in the old testament, the act of Jesus in giving the beloved disciple to be her son shows him clearly to represent the church, the collectivity of the disciples whom Jesus loves. The importance of this action is emphasised by the fact that it is immediately after this that we read 'After this, Jesus, knowing that all was now accomplished . . .' (19:28); it is the climax of Jesus' deeds on the cross, the climax of his 'hour', because it sets the church on its path, creating the community of love between those he loves.

The figure of the beloved disciple takes on additional significance in the resurrection stories if he is considered in this way, especially as he seems to have been inserted by John into narratives where he originally had no place and where John therefore saw him as conveying a special lesson (Raymund E. Brown p 1004, cf 922). It is the beloved disciple who comes to believe at the empty tomb and who on the lake recognises the risen Lord. In the parallel story of Peter's visit to the tomb in Lk

24:12, Peter is alone and fails to understand or find faith; even in John's version it does not seem that Peter understands at that moment. It is perhaps worth considering that it may be in reference to his generalised function as 'the disciple whom Jesus loves' that the saying about his remaining till Jesus comes was originally meant. It was only when this figure became too closely associated with a particular individual that the difficulty about his death arose (21:20-23). The evangelist wants to show that faith and understanding are the work of love, born of sensitive awareness and closeness to Christ rather than from mere seeing.

In this respect the lesson of the beloved disciple coincides with the final beatitude of the main body of the gospel: 'Happy are those who have not seen and yet believe' (20:29). At intervals throughout the gospel the evangelist has stressed the insufficiency of mere seeing and the need for spiritual insight in order to understand the message of Jesus and adhere to him. During Jesus' earthly life, when it is possible to see Jesus, it is of course primarily the negative side of this that is stressed, as when he complains, 'You will not believe unless you see signs and portents' (4:48), and where he is objecting to the mere viewing of wonders without understanding them (6:26). After Jesus has left his disciples, the other side, the spiritual insight, becomes all-important, and it is for this reason that the evangelist highlights the beloved disciple's loving responsiveness to Christ, and concludes with the beatitude which sets the tone for all future believers for whom the book is, as he says immediately afterwards, written: That you may believe that Jesus is the Christ, the son of God, and that believing you may have life in his name' (20:31).

The risen Christ in his church

Another theme prominent in John's resurrection stories
and of great importance for the community of the early
church is that of separation and return. That of
separation comes out in the story of the appearance to
Mary Magdalen. This meeting is reported also by Mt
28:9-10, but the words of Jesus are there different,
indeed almost functionless since they do no more than
repeat the message already given to the women by the
angel. It is quite possible that Matthew's tradition did
not include the content of the message but only the fact
that a message was given, and the evangelist supplied the
content from the previous message. John may well have
done the same, for his message is both wholly different
from anything in the other gospels and fully consonant
with his own theological emphases earlier in the gospel.
For John there are two principal senses to the moment
of the passion and resurrection of Jesus which together
form the 'hour' to which the whole gospel looks
forward (ever since 'my hour has not yet come' in 2:4);
it is the moment of glorification and the moment when
Jesus leaves his disciples to prepare an eternal home for
them. Throughout the gospel the hour of Jesus' passion
is looked forward to as the moment of his exaltation —
a typical Johannine ambivalent term, which includes in
its meaning the lifting up on the cross (3:14), the raising
up at the resurrection and the glorification at God's side
(12:32, 34; 17:1-5) — and the Johannine presentation
of the passion itself is in fact a royal triumph: Jesus
makes his captors fall back by a word, carries his cross
like a standard, and is recognised as king by Pilate's
inscription. But the triumph is still to be completed by

exaltation to God's side (17:5). This is the most likely
sense of Jesus' refusal to let Mary Magdalen cling to
him. All kinds of improbable explanations of this have
been proposed (his wounds were still sore; he was
naked) but the most likely is that this bit of dialogue is
a dramatic accompaniment of Jesus' following message
that he is ascending to the Father. Contrary to the
popular conception, fostered by the liturgical feast, that
the ascension of Christ was an event which took place
only forty days after the resurrection, the majority of
new testament texts unite in considering as one event
the resurrection and the exaltation at God's right hand.
It is only the Acts of the Apostles which mentions the
interval of forty days before the final separation of
Christ from his disciples, and the same author also
describes (Lk 24:51) a separation and exaltation to
heaven which appears to take place on the day of
resurrection itself. The import, then, of the dialogue
with Mary Magdalen is to underline that the glorification of Christ beside the Father is an integral part of
the resurrection.

But it teaches also about the effect of the exaltation
for Christ's followers. The formula 'I am ascending to
my Father and yours, to my God and yours' (20:17)
shows that the risen Christ takes his followers with him.
As a formula it recalls the expression by which Ruth
protests that she will enter into complete community
with her mother-in-law Naomi: 'Your people shall be
my people, and your God, my God' (Ru 1:16). It
suggests that here, too, there is to be total community
between Christ exalted and the disciples, thus rejoining
his saying at the supper, 'I am going to prepare a place
for you . . . so that where I am you may be also' (14:2).

It encourages the church, then, to keep its glance on the risen and exalted Lord, as already citizens of heaven, since his exaltation is only a prelude to theirs; as Paul has it, 'our citizenship is citizenship of heaven' (Phil 3:20).

Complementary to the theme of ascent is that of return. It was prominent in the final words of Jesus to his disciples before the passion in such sayings as 'A little while and you will no longer see me, and again a little while and you will see me' (16:16). Together with this series of sayings was another, promising that the holy Spirit will come to them as his representative to teach, guide and strengthen them on his behalf, and be their Paraclete (the word is a legal term exactly similar to 'advocate', one who is called to stand by and support a client who needs help). To the Hebrew mind this representative could almost be said to be Jesus himself. Although the modern mind would insist that they are two separate persons, their similarity of role and function gives them, to the semite, the same personality, for it is in a way the function which defines the identity. So Malachi can prophesy that Elijah will come again, and Jesus can say that he has come in the person of John the Baptist (Mt 11:14). Jesus himself can be represented in the gospel of Matthew as a second David or a second Moses because the return of both these great figures was prophesied and he fulfills the prophecies. In the same way the Spirit which continues Jesus' work makes him present and is his spirit in the fullest sense (the necessity of writing the word with a small or large 's' draws a distinction where none should be made; both senses are included).

Correspondingly the same teaching of the presence of

Jesus' spirit occurs also after the resurrection as part of the dispositions which the risen Lord makes for his community, when he breathes on them and says 'Receive the holy spirit'. This is the fulfilment of his promise (20:22). But his presence with them in their mission is in a way emphasised even more strongly by his charge 'As the Father sent me, so I am sending you' (20:21). The union of Jesus with his Father, and the fact that Jesus is doing only the work of him who sent him, have been often brought out in the course of the gospel, and now this union of sender and sent is transferred to the disciples. Thus the circle is completed: as the disciples are present with the risen Lord in his exaltation, so he is present with them in their mission on earth.

The two lessons about the future community are in a sense combined in Christ's dialogue with Peter after the meal by the lakeside. Until now it has been the beloved disciple who has represented and brought out the importance of the sensitivity of love, and it is to all the disciples that the Lord has given his spirit for their mission. In the dialogue with Peter they are combined because Christ gives Peter charge of his sheep only at the triple protestation of Peter's love. Not only does Peter's protestation repair his triple denial during the passion but further it shows that the union with Christ in love is an essential prerequisite for pastoral office in the church.

Christ the Lord

It is, as Raymund Brown points out (p 1032, 1047), not

by chance that the last words spoken by a disciple in the
gospel of John (before the addition of chapter 21, the
appendix) are Thomas' supreme profession of faith.
Brown regards the whole incident as a dramatisation oi
the theme of doubt turning to faith. The drama
certainly re-uses expressions which have already been
used for the previous appearance of Jesus, and so
suggests that it has been constructed by the evangelist in
imitation of this — an echo with a different message.
The message of the first appearance was the joyful
union of Christ and his disciples; alone of the resurrection appearances it remains unclouded by doubt or
hesitation. But the motif of doubt returns in full force
with Thomas; it is as though John has split into two the
appearance described in Lk 24:36-49, in order to bring
out the different motifs more clearly. Here there is
doubt, which appears only to be triumphantly overcome.

The significance of Thomas' confession can go unnoticed by a post-Nicene christian. Firstly its position is
prominent in the gospel as the final response of man,
especially because it arches over to rejoin the first verse
of the gospel in which the relationship of the Word to
God is already described 'and the Word was god'. The
small letter is used deliberately in an attempt to avoid
the confusion of the Word with God the Father or — in
the other direction — the understatement 'the Word was
divine'. Perhaps the best periphrasis is given by the New
English Bible: 'What God was, the Word was'. Secondly,
the rarity with which Jesus is called 'God' in the new
testament makes these two passages which bracket
John's gospel all the more striking. Raymund Brown
finds only one other passage (Heb 1:8-9) which clearly

calls Jesus 'God' apart from these two in John; even this is considerably less strong because it is dependent on a psalm verse, and such a literary allusion can often slightly influence or distort a writer's way of expressing himself ('Does the New Testament call Jesus God?' *Theological Studies 26,* 1965, p 545-573, published also in his *Jesus God and Man,* London, 1968.) Apart from these three, there exist only five other passages in the new testament in which there is a 'certain probability' that Jesus is given the title, all of which are doubtful on grounds of text or meaning (*Jesus God and Man,* p 28).

This lack of evidence for the use of the divine title for Jesus does not of course mean that he made no divine claims or that these claims went unregarded by the gospel. It only shows that to say of any man that he was God was to the Jews so staggering as to be almost meaningless; it was almost too baffling even to be blasphemous. Jesus' way of putting forward his true personality had, therefore, to be much more subtle: he claimed to do, and demonstrably did, actions which only God could do, such as forgiving sins, giving life and controlling the forces of nature. In John he suggests his divine quality more by speaking of his unique relationship with the Father and of his ability to do the works of the Father, and by the mysterious use of the phrase 'I am', recalling the self-designation of God to Moses at the burning bush (eg 8:24, 28:13:19). But these indications seem to have evoked no response of understanding on the part of the disciples, only of murderous hostility on the part of his opponents (8:58-59); the evangelist often comments that his disciples understood some word of Jesus only after the resurrection (2: 22; 7; 39). It took time, and above all the key of the resurrection, for the disciples to assimilate the significance of Jesus' words and actions, and to plumb the depths of their implications — indeed one may well ask whether the church has yet done so, or ever will do before the consummation of the world. The continued lack of understanding of the twelve even after the forty days till the ascension (Ac 1:6) suggests that Luke considers this to have persisted longer than John; but of course for Luke the moment of enlightenment comes with the dramatic scene of the coming of the Spirit at Pentecost.

In concluding his gospel with this full declaration of the divinity of Christ John does perhaps foreshorten. He represents Thomas as expressing with stark clarity what may well have been only dimly understood so soon after the startling event of the resurrection. But it is fitting that the gospel and the account of the risen Christ should conclude with a declaration of the full faith to which these events led and to which the evangelist will bring his readers.